THE UNIFIED LIFE THEORY

THE UNIFIED LIFE THEORY:

A Philosophy for Living

Tom DeBlois, P.Eng.

The Book Guild Ltd
Sussex, England

The Book Guild Ltd
25 High Street,
Lewes, Sussex

First published 1998

Set in Times
Typesetting by Raven Typesetters, Chester

Printed in Great Britain by
Bookcraft (Bath) Ltd, Avon

A catalogue record for this book is
available from the British Library

ISBN 1 85776 380 7

CHAIN BOOK
(similar to the old chain letter idea)

After you have read *The Unified Life Theory*, give this book to someone who you think may be interested in saving mankind and other animals from extinction. Or give it to someone who would want to encourage women to take charge of many aspects of life. Ask them please to send it on to others.

If you wish to re-read *The Unified Life Theory* you can always find it in your local library. Better still, if you are incredibly intelligent and hip, you could purchase another *Unified Life Theory* book and leave it out on your coffee table. Everyone else will then know how intelligent and hip you are.

CONTENTS

ACKNOWLEDGEMENTS

This is not a scholarly thesis embodying original research. It is merely an attempt to put into words ideas that have been developed from experiences over a long life, plus ideas gleaned from conversations, the reading of books, magazines and newspapers and from watching television. This book is intended for the general reader (preferably young adults who are able to question today's values and beliefs). It is hoped that you will find this philosophy simple and understandable, and that it will be your guide to answering questions about life.

Many of the ideas about marriage and children have come from school principals and teachers who have so many stories about children from dysfunctional families, divorced or separated parents, who can't be bothered, or don't know how, or just beat the kids anyhow.

This book in no way depicts my own marriage and children. I was extremely lucky in the quality of my wife and three children. Like any marriage we have had our problems and differences, but my wife has been with me now for over 55 years, and I wish to praise her for putting up with how I have changed over the years. She married a chap who was a member of the church choir and even taught Sunday school for three years when our children were young, but gradually I became more and more liberal. I stopped going to church because I finally could no longer believe. The biggest problem came when I wanted to become a nudist, but my wife's and my feeling for each other has been strong enough for us to continue to try to make each other as happy as possible. I am fortunate to have been married to a smart, most intelligent woman who has been a wonderful wife and especially a wonderful mother.

INTRODUCTION

Our present life-style produces an over-abundance of pollution and an existence that is too often full of misery, unhappiness, pain and suffering. The underlying reason for the lack of joy in living is because we continue to do the things that our genes and traditions have programmed us to do. The males have genes producing a strong desire to have intercourse, and females have good-mother genes. The success of this behaviour is obvious, but if it were to continue, our over-population would spell disaster.

Over-population is the basic cause of all our air and water pollution and the depletion of the world's natural resources, as well as the depletion and extinction of many animals, fish, birds and insects. The reduction of our population is mandatory if humans are to survive. The most important idea in the Unified Life Theory is that more people should cry out, 'Ban the bomb', not the nuclear kind, but the population kind. 'Ban the population explosion.' This is the only way to save the human race and all the other animals.

The breakdown of marriage and the family is understandable. Marriage was a good arrangement in order to support stay-at-home women with many children, but today, with working women and few children, the family is not at all best for children or parents. Since our society no longer requires marriage in order to have sex, and since marriage is the antithesis of freedom it is obvious that marriage is no longer recommended. The Unified Life Theory suggests a better extended family arrangement that would also accommodate and encourage the very necessary population reduction needed to save the human race from eventual extinction.

This new philosophy is based on the idea that humans are

animals subject to the laws of nature. We must use our superior brains to curb our genetic programming, and act according to what is logical and reasonable to create a much happier existence. Women must decide that having babies and raising children is not a God-given purpose in life, and is not as fulfilling as striving for their individual goals. Men wrote that women should 'be fruitful and multiply' because it was necessary in ancient times, but today women must take control of their professional, personal and sexual lives.

The Unified Life Theory uses logic and reason to suggest answers to questions concerning: the meaning of life; our goal in living; the purpose in life; life after death; the will of God; our moral code; sex; contraception; abortion; euthanasia; the death penalty; pollution; ecology; taxes; marriage; religion; ethnic groups; animals for research; genetic manipulation of humans; censorship; pornography; immigration; birth-rate and population; child-rearing; nudity; homosexuals and lesbians; gambling and drugs. What we need is a philosophy of life based on logic and reason.

Life would be so much better and simpler if we had a basis for knowing what was 'right' or 'wrong'. We should not have to be uncertain and have to make 'judgement calls'. Some religious people use the Bible as their basis; some use the Koran; some use the Talmud; some use many other ancient writings, and each human grouping has its own culture and standards and beliefs, all seeming to be so different, yet in fact so similar. However, most of the writings are so contradictory that, for instance, two people studying the Bible could come up with two different conclusions concerning contraception.

All were written so long ago that it is not logical to believe their philosophy for living would be best for conditions today. Traditional ideas and methods are not always the best. Some people look for guidance from a more modern religious writer, a TV evangelist, a more modern 'xspurt'. But remember that x (in algebra) stands for the unknown, and 'spurt' is a drip under pressure. Or an expert is a person 50 miles from home. In other words, all the experts in the world can't beat good common sense. If it's comfortable, use it. Use logic and reason.

So many of our guides for living are so complicated. Why can't we put the facts and questions into a simple formula that all can remember, and have the answer come out with no 'ifs, ands or buts'. It would be wonderful if a theory of life could be found which would be logical, rational, straight-forward, easy to follow and understand, and be a basis for answering all our questions.

The only way to find this theory is to look for some basic and fundamental ideas that are common to all the problems in life. In recent years this common denominator has been described by many, and you will now find it in the Unified Life Theory. (The title is to remind you of Albert Einstein's search for the Unified Field Theory that would answer all the questions regarding the fundamental forces of gravity, magnetism and electricity with one mathematical formula.)

The Unified Life Theory

1. Humans are animals who have developed an unusually sophisticated brain, a pair of dextrous hands with opposing thumb and fore-finger, and, like all animals, are subject to the laws of nature.
2. Life can be made much more enjoyable and interesting if logic and reason are used to suggest changes to our laws, beliefs, customs, conventions and way of life.
3. The purpose in life, or the goal in life, is that which our mind creates for us. The basic goal of all animals is to avoid pain and suffering and to find as much joy, happiness and contentment as possible. 'Life, liberty and the pursuit of happiness' is the goal of all animals. The new moral should be, 'good' is pleasure, 'bad' is pain.
4. Our population must be reduced to a suitable number in order to avoid air, water, and other pollution and to avoid the extinction of animals, fish, birds and insects. Women must take prime responsibility for population control by limiting births.
5. The human brain can over-ride its genetic programming.
6. 'Natural selection' is *not* improving the human body and mind, so selective breeding and genetic engineering should be used.

7. We should *not* try to prevent people from doing what they would like to do, as long as it does not hurt other people or damage their property.

Remember that the Unified Life Theory forms the basis to give humans a better quality of life and reasonable answers to all our questions, but only if all agree and live by its code. It might not be perfect, but it is far better and simpler than anything we have now. This is a 'formula for living'. Insert the problem into the formula and you can get an answer. Its correctness cannot be guaranteed, because it cannot be scientifically proven. However, the Unified Life Theory should stand the test of time, and the human race is probably doomed without it. That's a fact.

Are the answers suggested in the following chapters logical and reasonable? We should first decide what constitutes logic and reason, so let's examine what the scientific mind does to find answers. It all starts with an inquiring mind that tries to analyze the details. Some people see things as they are and say, 'Why?' – the analytical mind. Some people see things as they should be and say, 'Why not?' – the visionary.

Scientists have a deep-seated faith that the universe exhibits order and is basically simple. If something is claimed to be true, it must stand the test of repeatability, just like a scientific experiment, where other experimenters must get the same results. Whenever any aspect of something seems to grow tangled and complex, scientists can't help searching for some underlying order.

Sherlock Holmes said, 'When you have eliminated the impossible, whatever remains, however improbable, must be the truth.' It reminds us of Albert Einstein's conclusion that nothing can exceed the speed of light. He didn't experiment and discover it. He found that the only way his mathematical formulae would all agree with the known conditions was if he added in the fact that nothing could exceed the speed of light. However improbable, it must be true.

A scientist would enjoy solving the problem of how the fly stopped the train. A law of physics states that an object moving along a line must decelerate and come to a complete stop before it can reverse along that same line. In other words, before an object can reverse, it must go through zero speed. So, the fly travelling down the tracks and hitting the front of the train, and now going in the opposite direction, must have gone through zero speed. Since, when the fly hit the train, it stayed on the front of the train, does this mean that the fly stopped the train?

One, not too detailed, explanation is that the fly is like the tennis ball that hits a tennis racket. The strings stretch backward (decelerate) until they come to zero speed, and then accelerate the ball in the opposite direction. So the fly merely depresses a piece of metal of the train through zero speed, and then the metal regains its shape.

By the way, it's not easy to swat a fly by coming down on it, because a fly detects the change in air pressure and can easily fly away from the descending hand. The better way is to catch it in your hand by swinging your hand sideways very fast. A fly can't jump up, so it tries to fly away from your hand.

For all people, a logical mind is a great help in coping with our modern society. Logic is sometimes called 'vertical' thinking; if you don't have enough of something, it would be logical to add more. But doing the 'logical' thing, or acting in a 'logical' way is not always the best solution. A logical mind should lead to 'lateral' thinking, a creative approach to living.

Creativity is sometimes called 'lateral' thinking; if you don't have enough of something, it is creative to consider that something different is better than more of the same. Lateral thinking is stepping sideways and viewing the problem from another perspective.

For example: invitations to a formal party had been sent out with house number 219 instead of 217. Logic said to send out revised invitations or telephone each party. Lateral thinking suggested that on the big day the house numbers could be switched.

Another example: during the Civil War a General's small army was about to be attacked by a vastly superior force. His men expected him to do the usual and logical thing and order a retreat to save his army. And he normally would have, but first wondered if there were an alternative. He discovered that the enemy's munitions supplies had been brought up close behind the troops and decided to do the unexpected. He sent a company of cavalry around the enemy's right flank and succeeded in destroying all their supplies. When the enemy realized this, they knew they could not win, and retreated.

Another example: a chess player moved his Queen to where it could be taken, knowing that if he 'sacrificed his Queen' he could win.

Solving problems can be made easier if you learn some of the techniques developed. One is called 'exaggeration'. The idea is to carry the problem to extreme in order to get a different perspective. For instance, you might wonder why women seem to cross their legs when sitting down more often than men; if you think it might be due to the fact that women's hip joints are generally further apart than men's, exaggerate.

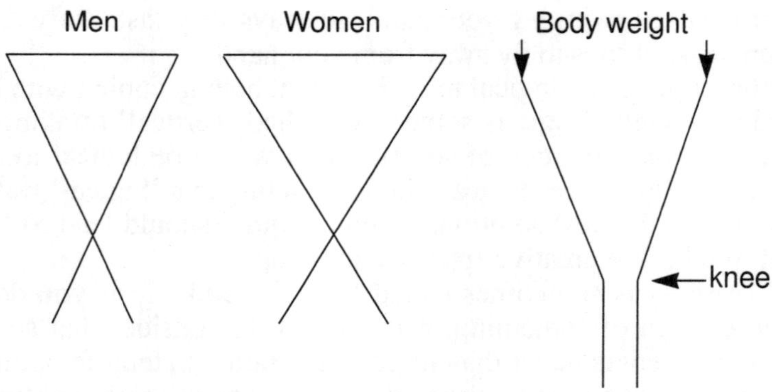

A man's legs would easily slide off, but a woman's wouldn't, because the angle is much greater. (When men cross their legs, they usually put one ankle on the opposite knee, but women don't very often, because they don't want it to appear that they are leaving their legs apart, as this is supposed to be a 'no-no'.)

Another example: have you ever noticed that a woman with wide hips has a greater angle between the leg bones above and below the knee than a man? Would there be a greater sideways force at the knee? Exaggerate (see diagram). Would this cause more knee problems for wide-hipped athletes?

Another example: if you should wonder if there is an advantage to foot-faulting (stepping forward over the base line) while serving in a tennis match, exaggerate.

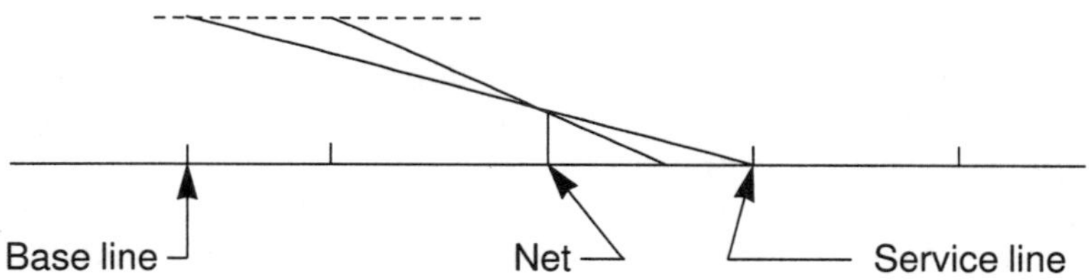

The closer to the net the ball is served, from the same height, the better the angle to get the ball in. Also if the ball is thrown up and in front, the server can hit the ball at a steeper angle in order to get the ball in.

Another technique is called 'similarities'. The idea is to find similar situations that tend to clarify a problem. For instance, if someone argues that we should not play God by having a death penalty, because it interferes with God's plan for that individual, search for examples where it has become acceptable to play God. You might think of the acceptability of doctors extending a person's life by means of a heart transplant.

Another example: in Ontario, it is not illegal for women to go topless, but some municipalities may want to remove topless women from public parks if someone objects because they are offended. You could argue that there shouldn't be any restriction for toplessness any more than there should be restrictions for weird hair-dos or a jewel hanging from a pierced tongue that offends many people equally.

Some people say that a smoker's medical bills should be paid by the tobacco company, but if we think of similar situations, we see how ridiculous it could be. Automobile manufacturers, for instance, would be expected to pay the medical bills for accident victims in their cars.

New ideas are necessary for adaptation and survival, so hopefully this attempt to apply logic and creativity to the problems of our society will be a guide to help humans form simplified answers to their everyday problems. So use reason and try your best to improve things. Analyze everything with logic.

One purpose of this book is to encourage people to realize that life for each of us can be so much more enjoyable and interesting if we search for ways to make things better, more useful, less time-consuming, faster, less expensive, or safer. The way to do this is to make a point of analyzing your surroundings and consider what would be more logical or rational.

Over the centuries many beliefs have been handed down from generation to generation, but there was no solid evidence that they were true. In many cases we simply believed them to be true because we wanted them to be true.

Many beliefs have been shown to be not true, or assumed to be illogical and therefore not to be believed: the world is not flat; ghosts and witches are not real; Unidentified Flying Objects are not outer-space-vehicles piloted by little green men; astrology and faith-healing are only believed by those who are not willing to take charge of their own lives; psychics and fortune-tellers cannot tell your future. And today we know that the picture of the Loch Ness Monster was a hoax.

All of the beliefs and way of life handed down to us must be put on the agenda to be questioned by applying logical thinking, lateral thinking, exaggeration and similarities. According to the English poet William Blake, 'The man who never alters his opinion is like standing water, and breeds reptiles of the mind.' A receptiveness to change is the key to positive growth.

To give equal status to men and women, simplified words should be used to take the place of the cumbersome he/she, him/her, Sir/Madam, and the possessive his/her. Our language didn't have the need for both gender words in so many cases, because it was a man's world. We had postmen, firemen, chairmen and foremen, because these jobs were always male. But not today, so we need some simple words to indicate a human being without indicating gender.

The new words should be respectively ee, hei, nam and ee's. Ee merely uses the last letter of both he and she. Hei combines the letters that are common in him and her. Nam uses the three common letters of 'man' and 'woman' in reverse order, and can also be used in place of Sir/Madam. The possessive is merely adding an apostrophe s to ee. These new words will be used throughout this book, but they will be underlined to emphasize their newness. Examples: Ee who hesitates is lost; Let hei who is without sin cast the first stone; Dear Nam; Ee's love of life.

'he/she'	becomes 'ee'
'him/her'	becomes 'hei'
'sir/madam' and 'man/woman'	becomes 'nam' (plural = 'nem')
the possessive 'his/her'	becomes 'ee's'
'waiter/waitress'	becomes 'waitree'

Everyone likes to have ee's routine. It is comfortable. You don't have to make decisions. You can go along your merry way knowing that you will be happy. But you should leave yourself open to change, because in some cases the change can be for the better.

'A Different Drummer'

Why should we be in such desperate haste
To succeed, and in such desperate enterprises?
If a nam does not keep pace with ee's companions,
Perhaps it is because ee hears a different drummer.
Let hei step to the music which ee hears,
However measured or far away.

So, be yourself. Like yourself. If you don't do your thing, it won't get done. What we need are more random acts of kindness, such as more pick-up bugs to compensate for all the litter-bugs.

HUMANS ARE ANIMALS

Not many people believe the Adam and Eve story about the beginning of humans. When ancient peoples had visions, they thought they were insights from God into events that they did not understand. Each group had a different explanation for the beginning of life, but all assumed the many unique forms could not have developed by chance, and that God, therefore, must have been the designer.

But how logical is it to think that our whole existence is a happenstance? Let's take a look and see how reasonable the assumed process is. Remember, mutations which survive are those that thrive under the laws of nature, natural selection, survival of the fittest. So there really is 'design'. The 'laws of nature' are the designer.

People used to wonder about how long it would take mutations to change, from one animal shape into a completely different shape, until they realized just how long a billion years was. When you realize that 1 million is a thousand times longer than 1 thousand, and 1 billion is a thousand times longer than 1 million, you realize animals have been on this earth a long time.

It is assumed now that the earth was formed 5 billion to 20 billion years ago, and that it took over 3 billion years for the first life to appear. It took another billion years for the first animals to appear, and then it took 1 billion years to get to today's humans. From the time of the first bony fish, it took 250 million years for the dinosaurs to appear.

Dinosaurs roamed the earth for 150 million years, whereas upright man has been here for 5 million years. It took 50 million years, after the calamity that wiped out the dinosaurs, for primates to be developed, and another 45 million years for upright primates to appear.

Let the earth's circumference of 40,000 km represent one billion years

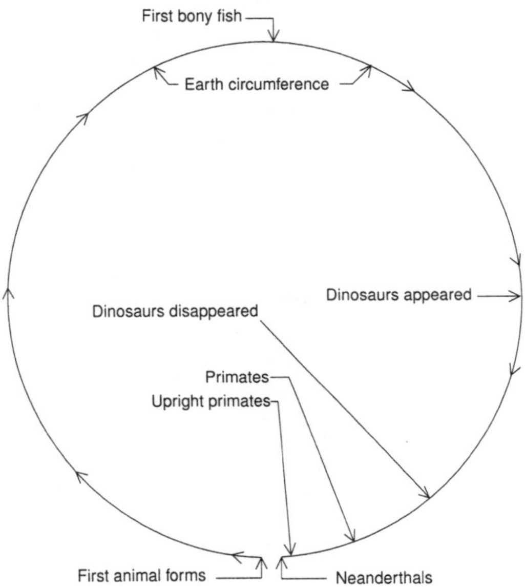

[Figures are approximate]

5,000,000,000	years ago Earth was formed (the big bang)	
2,000,000,000	First life forms	
1,000,000,000	First animal forms	40,000 km
500,000,000	First bony fish	20,000 km
250,000,000	Dinosaurs appeared	10,000 km
100,000,000	Dinosaurs disappeared	4,000 km
50,000,000	Primates appeared	2,000 km
5,000,000	Upright primates	200 km
500,000	Neanderthals appeared	20 km
50,000	Homo Sapiens appeared	2 km
15,000	The last ice age	600 m
5,000	Egyptians	200 m
2,000	Christ born	80 m
100	Wright brothers flew	4 m
1	Last year	4 cm

If you can picture the circumference of our earth (40,000 km) as representing 1 billion years, then 4 cm equals 1 year. If you could walk (west) back in time, from the Kennedy Space Center, Florida, 4 cm per year, you would be back when the first upright primates were on the earth when you reached the Gulf Coast (200 km). All the rest of the world's circumference represents the development of the animals up to upright primates.

The first dinosaurs were probably animals larger than the lizards, and over the 150 million years they grew larger and larger. One wonders how some of these large animals could survive. What is the explanation for how the very long-necked plant-eater, the barosaurus, was able to breathe? Ee's long neck was certainly enough to reach the lush new sprouts of the trees and tall shrubs, but how did ee get fresh air down that long neck into ee's lungs with only one windpipe? When humans breathe out, stale air is left in the windpipe, and when we take a breath, the stale air in the pipe must come back into the lungs before any fresh air gets there. Stale air still has oxygen in it, so we don't need very much fresh air to give our lungs a satisfactory mix. Fresh air has 21% oxygen and 0.04% carbon dioxide. Exhausted air has 16% oxygen and 4% carbon dioxide. A deep breath brings a large proportion of fresh air, because the distance between our nose and lungs is short.

With a long neck it would seem that the lungs' expansion capacity would have to be very great, or maybe the breathing tube itself was able to transfer oxygen. Maybe the long-necked barosaurus had two windpipes and valves so that one windpipe was for breathing in fresh air, and one windpipe was for breathing out stale air.

That's not a bad idea. An athlete or a person with emphysema, who needs fresh air should have a tube inserted into ee's trachea (the breathing tube) just above the lungs. A valve in the tube would allow fresh air in but prevent air from going out. Valves in the nostrils, to allow air out but not in, would not be required, because the throat can close the nose passage while breathing in. This arrangement allows the use of the voice as well as breathing in and out through the mouth if desired. Some day this procedure might be as common as breast implants are today.

From upright primates to the present is 5 million years. From upright primates back to the first primates is not just double the 5 million years, it is ten times that, and it is another ten times that to get back to bony fish. If there were only 10 mutations per year, 50 million years would see 500 million mutations. You should now be able to picture how this was enough time to develop not only humans but all the other creatures. Did you know that the manatee and the elephant came from a common ancestor?

You might also ask how an organ, such as the eye, could be developed by a series of chance mutations. You might argue that every intermediate step in the development of an organ must enhance the survival of its owner, and because only the completed eye is of any use, then the eye could not have evolved. Doesn't this prove that the eye would need a designer? Well, yes, but the only designer needed is the 'laws of nature'.

Let's see how it works. The early mutations would cause some skin to be sensitive to light in such a way as to allow the animal to distinguish between night and day, similar to the one-celled plants that are able to move toward the light and therefore stay alive. The next mutations for animals would be to form a cup with a more sensitive lens at the opening which can discern movement. Each change would have to help form a more accurate optical image, and the process would be complicated. But, according to a computer program, it would take less than 2,000 changes, and maybe 500,000 years to accomplish. In evolutionary terms this is no time at all.

Another thought that suggests that enough time has elapsed to allow for sufficient mutations to have occurred to produce humans is the time it would take for continental drift to have taken place. For North and South America to have drifted away from Africa, at the rate of maybe the width of three fingers each year, would have taken what seems like a long time.

One mutation which has occurred in our lifetime is that humans have become taller. Another is the birth of an almost white-skinned child from black parents. If we assume that all humans descend from the upright 'Lucy' in Africa, then there must have been some white skins who were driven out to the north and some yellow skins who were driven out to the east. Brown-skinned and black-skinned people of Africa probably survived to some extent because their skin colour was a good camouflage in the jungle. In the north, the white people's skin colour did not matter so much because they wore clothing to keep warm, and the woods were not as dark.

What happened to the green humans? We have red, white, brown, black and yellow humans now, but maybe some mutations were of other colours and were killed off or died off. Bones of many animals have been found that are different than those of the animals we have today, but there must be countless varieties that have not been found. Today we have the most unusual golden-coloured hammerhead sharks and blue lobsters.

When you realize that there were few forms to start with, probably fish, there must have been many in between before we got to alligators, birds, mammals, insects, etc. So many must have died out. Many unusual forms may have prospered for a while but were killed off or their habitat changed so they could not survive. Maybe too many green-skinned males preferred to have intercourse with males, and with too few babies, green people died out.

The animal species that survived have developed successful features: lions are strong and have strong jaws; spiders make webs; skunks spray. Humans survived because of their brain, their dextrous hands and their ability to communicate. We were probably good at killing off many who, if they had prospered, might have been quite different. They may have been like the Martians we picture today. They could have had eyes that see in the dark and are set further apart, giving better binocular vision; eyes on the ends of extensions that could see around corners and behind; heads that could turn 180 degrees like an owl's; a tail to use as another arm; or a tail to wag to show pleasure. Just think of the desirable features we may have destroyed.

If nature had been kind to humans, we would have had skin so tough that it would be difficult for mosquitoes to penetrate; lungs that would let us stay underwater a long time like whales; legs that could run as fast as a cheetah; a nose that could smell like a dog's; ears that could hear higher frequencies; intestines that didn't have an appendix to get infected; a spinal column more suited to upright activities; lungs not subject to asthma; joints not subject to arthritis; injuries or problems not signalled by pain, but by some less hurtful means, such as light coming on or a sound going off; brains that could calculate and do maths as fast and accurately as a computer; teeth that were straight, looked nice, and had a good bite; blood vessels as strong as nylon; a bowel movement that wasn't painful; skin that changed colour to reflect hot sun or turned dark at night to conserve heat.

Just think about what we might have been. Certainly our bodies are not the best. Mark Twain once observed: 'Man seems to be a poor rickety sort of thing. He is always undergoing repairs. A machine that was as unreliable as him would have no market.'

Some tend to think of animals as having special features that were developed that way because they wanted or needed the feature to survive. But mutations are quite random. Some features are: of no help or value; a hindrance to survival; a help in survival or give pleasure in life.

The offspring of some mammoths had more hair than the average, and as the ice-age temperatures grew colder, the hairier offspring thrived better and had more offspring. Before long we had the woolly mammoth. If the woolly mammoth had also developed a good brain along with something like fingers on its trunk (or maybe more than one trunk), it might have destroyed nam's beginnings and become the dominant creature. As it happened, it could not adapt when the ice-age ended and is now extinct. There are many human features that did not disappear during ee's development, such as baldness. Now with hair-pieces, bald men will continue to sire children.

If the human form is in God's image, it doesn't say much for God, especially when you consider the female body with internal organs that give her pain and suffering and a mess every month, and the emotional and physical problems of menopause, such as mood changes, hot flashes, lack of energy, and lack of sleep. Females would prefer not to have breasts the size of melons, and hips too wide for energetic activity.

Males are attracted by the sight of wide hips; breasts; smooth, hairless skin; soft and delicate features, coupled with a show of willingness. In the past, more of this type had babies, and as a result these features were accentuated over the generations. Females who tended to be domineering probably did not attract as many males, so what we ended up with were females who were weak and submissive.

Luckily, the males must have been strong enough to protect the females and babies from predators, or otherwise our species would not have survived. This is genetic programming. We are what we are by what has been handed down through generations, but our brains can free us if we think about what is desirable.

Humans are just one of the billions of animal and insect life-forms on this planet. A better brain allowed us to develop fire and tools to build shelter against the cold. We have survived because our ancestors, over thousands and millions of years, have been genetically changed in ways that made them better at surviving than many other forms.

However, humans are really no better than many other forms of life which we were not in competition with, such as sharks, ants, birds, etc. We are not the most populous of life-forms. We are not as well adapted to survive the future as are mice, cockroaches and grasshoppers. We just happen to be the best at building and killing.

History suggests that people not of one's own group were held to be inferior, evil and dangerous, especially if they were outwardly different in appearance. Our ancestors must have killed off a lot of the 'different' people in order for today's humans to be so much alike.

We have been a factor on the earth for a very short time, but in that time we have completely changed the physical world, and our over-population is gradually destroying most other life-forms. Our population has grown to the point where we are approaching a calamity. When we think about how our race should proceed to avoid the calamity and to develop a happier life for all, we must consider who we are, how we got to where we are, and where we want to go.

Life, according to the dictionary, consists of the metabolism of protoplasm to produce energy, growth, reproduction and adaptation to the environment. The two main forms of life are plants and animals. Since most plants can get along without animals, we assume plants came first. Can you imagine the number of mutations that had to occur for the first water plants to become the grasses, vegetables, weeds, flowers, bushes, and finally the trees we have today? When you consider that only the fittest plants survived, it becomes obvious that many have died. The same is true of animals.

Just think. It's taken 5 million years to go from the first upright nam to the present nam. That took a lot of mutations and changes, and it's only been about 15,000 years since most humans were living in caves and still fighting other humans for territory or other gains.

Nem have been fighting each other all during recorded time. Examples include Genghis Khan; the Greeks; the Romans; the killing off of so many Indians in the new world; the many revolutions; the World Wars.

Mankind has not had time yet to change genetically from the aggressive predator. But we have made some progress. We now say that burning witches and the slave trade were inhuman, meaning that our brain is starting to overcome some of our animal instincts. We are predators, and only by using our brains will we be able to develop a social system to get along with one another.

It is important to know where we have come from before we can try to suggest what life will be like in the future. What humans think and do is largely dependent on heredity, our genes, and on our socialization (what we learn through our environment).

If the human body evolved to fit a certain lifestyle, we should study our ancestors' lives to find out what they ate, how much exercise they got, and what their lifestyle was like. However, we should realize that our bodies and our genetic programming have not changed much, but our lifestyle and social organization has changed dramatically. The world our genes 'think' we live in is nowhere near the world today.

Because of our superior brain, we now understand how bodies can be changed in a reasonable time, by developing breeding patterns and genetic engineering to produce humans that are much better suited to our modern world. Our bodies are not going to change very much as long as couples can have as many babies as they want, regardless of how beautiful or ugly, or clever or stupid, or imperfect they are.

WHY BELIEVE IN GOD?

Having a religion is comforting. It gives one the feeling of being loved, special, dignified, proud of being human. It gives organization, a feeling of togetherness, goals to strive for, and a feeling of self-worth. Each religion teaches guidelines for living, the moral and ethical rules, such as being honest, trustworthy, loyal, courteous, kind, obedient, cheerful, brave, clean and reverent. Religious people do good works and are a support for those who are depressed or for those who are suffering. They need to feel close to a supreme being, and they need to have the association of their church, the cornerstone of their existence.

Many derive a great deal of comfort from their prayers and their pouring out of their feelings to their God. They derive a spiritual sustenance from the church service and their belief is sustained just by being in church. To them the contemplation of the divine, the reality of the unseen, is a powerful force. It is real to them. It is nice for those who believe in the soul to feel that the one who has passed away is not really totally gone, that ee's soul lives on and is watching over us, giving us strength and encouragement.

The Unified Life Theory does *not* wish to discourage this. If it works, if it is good, by all means keep your faith. However, this does *not* include the acceptance that what was written in the bible or other religious works is the word of God. Nor does this accept the idea that the existence of the soul demands that life is sacred and should *not* be tampered with. You should not use your faith to prevent others from doing what they want to do, including the death penalty, euthanasia, etc.

The Unified Life Theory suggests that it is logical *not* to believe in God or gods who interfered in our present universe. It is logical *not* to believe in a life after death. It is logical *not* to believe in a God-given goal or purpose in life.

The following is for those who feel they are swamped by the number of people around the world who believe in a God who interferes in our present universe. They feel religion should be subject to the same critical analysis as an investigation of UFOs. The following is an attempt to show some of religion's good and bad features and how illogical some of its reasoning is.

Children learn about God from their parents and from Sunday school, and are conditioned to believe in God by rituals such as prayers, baptisms, communions, weddings, funerals, or kneeling with head to ground facing Mecca each day at certain hours. These are routines which imprint themselves on the individuals in order to condition them in the religious beliefs. This is strong medicine and is sure to hold their attention. Everyone is conditioned by so many people talking about God.

Some religious people are fundamentalists who say they believe everything in 'the book'. They feel that religious writings are the 'word of God', and that everyone should live according to the prophet's interpretation of 'the word'.

Others, 'the faithful', believe that life is sacred, that God interferes with events to help the deserving (divine intervention), that their prayers can make a difference, and that God speaks to them in many ways. They say the prophets were men who were influenced by their environment as they tried to interpret what they heard from God. In many cases their writings misinterpreted what God had in mind, and therefore the faithful choose not to believe everything. They do have a 'reverence for life' and believe that human intelligence is insufficient to understand God's great design. They feel that each and every person has a soul, and that this sets hei apart from the animals. When asked to give a definition of their faith, they might answer, 'Faith is the willingness to stand or fall by the noblest hypothesis.'

'The faithful' think fundamentalists are people who will believe almost anything, and are not willing to study the bible to find the true meaning. It doesn't occur to 'the faithful' that they are picking and choosing what they wish to believe in order to make life as they would like it to be. They believe in a soul and after-life, because they want an after-life, but wanting it does not make it true. If they believe any of the ideas that could not be, according to the laws of nature, they are just as liable to be wrong as the fundamentalists.

The bible says Jesus was born of a virgin. 'The faithful' choose not to believe this, because it is not reasonable. If they believe so much is not true, how can they decide what is true? If they used the same reasoning, they would conclude that the idea that Jesus had communication with God was an exaggeration, not to be taken literally.

Still others believe only in God, and maybe a purpose in life, and maybe an after-life. Most of these people have questioned established religion, but don't seem to feel that anything else makes sense. They are infuriated by the silence of God, and they feel 'as flies to wanton boys are we to the Gods'. But surely God would not have made nam go through life without a soul that has a reward in an after-life. They feel it doesn't make sense that there is no purpose in life.

Many people don't leave their religion for fear of feeling adrift without something to hold on to. When they do think of the possibility of there being no God, no soul and no after-life, they can find no theory of life that would be at all satisfying. But if these people would talk to some Humanists, they would be likely to find what they are looking for.

There are millions of Humanists worldwide who have rejected all belief in God and the supernatural. They suggest a way of life that revolves around rational free thought that relies on human intelligence rather than on divine guidance. They believe that the meaning of life is to be found in what each person puts into it. They feel that: 'The good life is one inspired by love and guided by knowledge.'

Surely people can't believe that a God cares about us when Ee would create a painful world of animals (including humans) who must kill and eat each other in order to stay alive; animals who, every few minutes, are in some kind of mental or physical pain; animals who are hurt, maimed or killed because of natural happenings, such as earthquakes, hurricanes, tornadoes, floods, pestilence; human animals who have the worry of growing up in a hectic modern world. No wonder people wanted to believe in a heaven, the great escape.

Some churches teach a rigorous strait-jacket of inhibitions and restrictions: you are condemned to everlasting hell and damnation if you don't believe; we will stay in hell (the great rebuke) forever for something we did wrong, unless forgiven; loose women provide occasions for sin. 'Thou shalt not' looms larger than 'please enjoy'. Belief in God is a deterrent to pleasure. There is a monkey on your back if you believe in God.

They talk about the beauty and goodness in the world as if it could only come from God, but they ignore the ugly and hateful suffering, fear and loneliness in the world, or attribute this to another type of God called the devil. What an awful way to go through life.

God seems to demand a great deal of attention, praise, adoration and thanks from people in their prayers, church attendance, and, at one time, sacrifices of animals or humans. Why should we be a 'sacrifice unto thee, oh Lord'? A God who requires that kind of attention has a psychological problem.

If God is such a super being, how come Ee's communication with humans has been through some kind of thought waves, which are so nebulous and indistinct that people can only guess the meaning? It's much more logical not to believe. Just think, you wouldn't have to try to dream up answers to a thousand questions, and living would be so much simpler.

Most ancient civilizations had their God or gods in their religion. This is understandable, because so much of life was magical and mysterious to them. Ancient people had to have 'fudge factors' to cover the immensity of their ignorance. What lay ahead was beyond their comprehension, so they invented deities and spirits and intermediaries such as medicine men, goddesses, shamans, and seers, who could interpret the ways of the spirits, the forerunners of priests and divine kings.

They believed that heavenly bodies were pushed by angels, and the wind was the breath of a storm god. They had to appease the gods of lightning, shooting stars and thunder to avoid crop failure and drought, and to obtain fertility in animals and their own families. They believed if they gave animal or human sacrifices to the god of war, of the harvest, or of life, or even asked them for help, that the gods would respond if their cause was just. They must have had a sufficient number of successes to keep their faith alive, but probably no more than our present day normal success rate.

Throughout history the belief in various spirits or gods was discarded after it was found that appeasing the gods did not change anything. The reason is that there is no solid or even good evidence that the physical laws of nature and science have ever changed or even been tampered with or altered for even a second. Every time science, or the understanding of the laws of nature, explained some of the mysteries, most believers in God accepted the explanation, but still kept their belief in God in order to account for other mysteries.

Other animals don't have brains capable of considering the existence of a God (we assume) but get along just fine. Just because we have a superior brain that can dream one up, that doesn't mean there is a God. This feeling of a spirit or a God may have been genetically programmed into all of the human animals, but by now our brains should over-ride this programming with logic. As there is order in nature, so should our thinking be orderly. Our quest should be to look for order.

So many people have claimed to be God's messengers, or to have been sent by God. However, just because Jesus is said to have had a special relationship with God, is no reason to believe that there is a God. A few, like Buddha, Mohammed and Jesus are still believed, but most, over the thousands of years, like Jim Jones, and more recently David Koresh, have been found to be charlatans or just deluded fanatics. Jim Jones convinced his flock that God wanted them to poison themselves and their children. David Koresh said he was God and ended up in a fiery holocaust with many followers.

Many enthusiastic leaders were martyrs who gave their lives for their cause, and they all felt they were hearing from God. But none of it makes sense when you think that all the prophets of all the religions were hearing such different things. How can people believe what the bible says about Jesus, when all of it is hearsay evidence written scores of years after his death. No judge would allow such evidence. People's minds will eventually help them to drop the idea of a God, and they will be a happier lot.

There is no reason why people should not think of Jesus, Mohammed, Buddha, or others, as good leaders. Many were martyrs who promoted the idea that we all should be kind and helpful to one another, but the ideas of the Unified Life Theory are better.

If there is no God, think of the waste of time and effort that has gone into serving God; doing God's will; deciding what parts of the bible were inspired by God, and how much is just the philosophy of the human who wrote it; converting non-believers; the crusades that killed so many; hunting down and burning the witches; the billions of sermons to many more billions of church goers; the building of elaborate temples, churches, monuments, pyramids and statues; and the conducting of intricate ceremonies. Think of all the dollars spent, all to please the gods.

More wars have been inflicted on people in the name of 'The Prince of Peace' than for any other reason. Religion itself is good for our society except where religion leads people to hate or be intolerant or try to make others follow its customs and beliefs.

It's so frustrating. Why not start with no beliefs, and then believe only what seems to have been proven, such as the laws of nature? It's so simple, logical, uncomplicated and satisfying. It is mostly the religious people who believe in psychics, ghosts and spirits. So don't believe in revelations and mystical experiences. Believe only in cause and effect, the simple laws of nature, the Unified Life Theory.

We assume that other animals don't think about God, but somewhere along the line some human animals did. Way back then ee also thought up the idea that nam was something far more special than other animals. The idea of being special solidified into the idea that humans had something that the animals didn't, a spirit that existed somewhere after the body died.

This is evident from the ancient bodies found buried with earthly goods to be used in the after-life. The after-life was associated with God who was in charge of heaven as well as earth. Today, we call this spirit the soul. This idea has lasted for thousands of years, and is one of the dominant features in all religions, and yet there is no good evidence that souls exist.

To believe in the soul requires a leap of faith to overcome the improbable. What is it? At what stage in our development did a soul come to humans and not other animals? Was it there when we first made fire? When does a newborn child get its soul? Do all female eggs have souls? Where do souls come from? Does God have an infinite supply, or does Ee make one when required, and out of what? When does a soul leave the body – after the heart stops; when the brain stops working; when the last rites are read? Does the soul pop back if CPR is successful?

What is it that survives after death? Is it how you were when you were young, when you were a wild teenager, or when you were old and miserable, or all three? Do you assume that your essence doesn't change? How will other souls in heaven recognize you? Will you be how you were when you were friendly and happy, or when you were bitter and ugly? You also have to assume that your soul has some kind of memory of events in your life so you will recognize other souls.

If humans feel that there must be an after-life, they had better be prepared to share it with all the animals and insects that have died, because there is no good reason to believe we are so special. You would also have to share the after-life not only with your dear departed, but with all the rapists, murderers, thugs, muggers and the guy next-door that you didn't like. What would an after-life as a soul, be like? Can you imagine anything that would not be boring as hell? This life is bad enough. Who would want another?

Your soul goes to heaven or hell depending on whether you have been 'good' or 'bad', according to God's judgement. God's 'good' and the devil's 'evil' are battling for the possession of your soul. What silly things our ancestors dreamed up. We can be good without God, and we can be bad without the devil.

All this because you are told that there is a spiritual nature to nam which animals don't have. Nam out-distances all other animals in linguistic ability, thought and reason. The differences, impressive as they are, are matters of degree, not of kind. The human's thinking brain is really the basis of our spiritual feelings.

There is no harm in believing in God and the after-life as long as you do not use the soul as a reason to prevent abortion and the death penalty. However, believing in souls and after-life is like believing in Martians, although according to our known physical laws they could not travel in space ships at the speed of or faster than the speed of light, and then stop and accelerate to high speed in a fraction of a second.

Religious people believe that we are special, because we are better than animals; we are God's chosen; we are made in God's image; we are so many and so dominant over other living things. But so were the dinosaurs in their day. We don't know what kind of brains they had, but if they were thinking about their standing in the world, they might have felt they were special, and maybe even God's chosen. Their kind certainly were dominant for a long time – a lot longer than our puny time on earth.

If God created all the animals equal, why would Ee consider humans to be so special and deserving of a soul when Ee allowed humans to destroy so many of God's creatures? It is not logical to think that God, after billions of years of evolution should reach down and give souls to only one species, especially one that is destroying so much of the earth and one that is likely to pollute the world, killing all living things.

Back in the time of Jesus, or back in the time of the Egyptian Pharaohs, people were happy to hear and believe that humans, or some humans, were God's chosen over all other animals. Today we would call this a prejudice, just as destructive and unfounded as the German Nazis' prejudice against Jews, and the whites' prejudice against blacks and others. The line between faith and fanaticism is faint.

Belief in a heavenly hereafter is supposed to be so wonderful, but it breeds religious fanatics who become terrorists who, like Japan's kamikaze pilots of World War Two, believe that to die in their holy war is to go straight to heaven. It's little wonder that people can be talked into the possibility of an after-life, when the religions have taken so much pleasure out of life here on earth. Believing in a soul for each person causes many problems. It's best to leave souls out of the picture. Yes, we are special, but we live and die just like other animals.

Quite a few people have had a near death experience – NDE – that they say proves the existence of an after-life. Well, if you believe that, you must also believe the people who say they were taken by little green men into a space ship, a so-called unidentified flying object, or UFO. The people who relate these events undoubtedly did experience something, but that is no reason to believe that something actually happened that would be contrary to the laws of nature.

These people most likely had a sleep experience where their dream memories were locked into their real-time memory. They say it wasn't a dream, because they remember it really happening. This is a known phenomenon which has been documented by having people observed while asleep. When awake, they tell about what happened to them when they were awake, when obviously they had been asleep.

Almost everyone can remember their dreams to some extent, which proves that dreams are actually in your memory. Some can relate their dreams hours later, but remember that it was a dream. It seems that some remember dreams as being in real-time, thus explaining UFOs and NDEs.

Most people have had the experience of dreaming that they are kicking a ball, and their leg actually kicks out and hits their spouse sleeping beside them. Normally, during your REM dream-time, your muscles are paralyzed or not receiving the signals they would normally receive when you are awake and thinking the same thoughts as in your dream. How often have you found your child screaming and crouching at the head of the bed, trying to get away from the monster. It takes time to convince the child that ee's been dreaming. How often, when in bed asleep, have you heard your spouse call out: 'I'm home.' You jump out of bed only to find the car not in the drive-way and spouse not home. Dreams often get switched into real-time.

All religions proclaim that the whole of life is in God's hands, and the Higher Intelligence knows what is best for us. A religious writer said that a prayer is always answered, but the answer comes according to the will of God, 'according to a higher Law of Love than our earthbound eyes can see.' 'Prayer is simply "Thy will be done" in any particular situation.'

Well, if God is going to do it Ee's way anyhow, Ee doesn't need your prayers to tell Hei 'Thy will be done.' But the religious writer immediately goes on to say that prayer can influence God to save some individuals, or that prayer can help the sick to fight to stay alive (presumably to thwart God's will). Honestly, do you really believe Ee will change the laws of nature just to help an individual live longer?

The religious writer refers to a double-blind experiment on coronary-care patients where half were prayed for regularly. Those prayed for were 'less likely to need antibiotics, to develop pulmonary oedema, or need intubation', and fewer died. Not 'none' you will note, and furthermore, no mention was made of the experiments where the results were just the opposite.

In any case, if God is going to cure some and not others 'according to a higher Law of Love', what makes you think prayer will change God's mind and ensure Ee does not proceed according to the Love Law? It is all too complicated to believe, but it is comforting to think that God thought enough of you to save your life. However, it is not so nice when Ee lets another die, just because there is no-one to pray for them. What kind of a God is this?

Many people still believe that God saved them from some calamity or was instrumental in putting them in position of great joy, but there is no reason to attribute these to a God now, any more than it was correct in ancient times. It puts the responsibility on someone else when nam alone is responsible for ee's actions, and there is a great deal of chance and luck.

Many people have felt that they have had thoughts as though someone outside themselves were giving them guidance. They have attributed this to God, and no one will ever prove to them that it wasn't, but no one will ever be able to prove that it is true.

If you feel that God decides on the outcome of many events, you will always feel frustrated in not knowing the logic or reasoning behind the decision, or why this event was chosen to be interfered with. To say: 'I have faith' will give you no satisfaction.

When a child dies, fundamentalists say: 'It is God's will', or 'It is part of God's plan', or 'God wanted the baptized child in heaven.' (Babies who died without having been baptized went into 'limbo', a world located between heaven and hell.) This is ridiculous. The child died because of an accident or germ. Some survive. Some don't.

There is no evidence that God answers prayers, talks to us,

interferes in our lives, or makes things happen or not happen, in contravention of nature's laws. What people see as God's intervention are coincidences. Believing in a God who does good things for people is as logical as believing in Santa Claus who comes down chimneys and brings presents to all good boys and girls, all over the world in one night, yet is never seen.

A lady buying a painting from a chap in Jakarta, Indonesia, who spoke a little English, was asked where she was from. When she said Toronto, Canada, his face lit up, and he said he knew a man from Toronto who had been kind to him, who lived on Stibbard Avenue. The friend's name was Morice Nichol, her next door neighbour. Coincidences happen all the time.

One man related how God spoke to him when he was trying to decide whether to go up to a house and knock on the door. He had been asking God for guidance, and was humming a tune, and when he got closer to the house he heard someone inside playing the same tune on the piano. He took that to be a message from God to knock on the door. He could not believe that this was coincidence, or, more likely, that he had heard the tune some distance away from the house and started to hum the tune without being aware of why.

A movie star, who was on drugs after his mother died and his wife had been murdered, was thinking about God while having breakfast alone in a coffee shop. A boy with a white jacket, blond curls and white shining teeth, came up and said: 'Jesus Christ loves you very much,' then went into the kitchen. The actor didn't know what to make of it, and finally got up and asked the hostess if he could talk to the blond chap in the kitchen. She said there was no blond boy, so he looked, and found none. He realized that he had been visited by an angel, and looking to a power higher than himself, he prayed, 'Father, come into my life. I have sinned. I cannot make it without you. Please help me off drugs.'

What the actor saw could have been a dream translated into his real-time memory, but even if it was a ghost, there is no reason to believe the ghost was sent by a God who is specifically interested in humans.

There is no way of knowing that God helped you to survive a sickness. You may have been praying to <u>Hei</u> and talking to <u>Hei</u>, and you may feel that Ee gave you the strength to fight on, but God didn't actually talk to you or give you any directions.

You feel you have gotten some help, because you feel different after you pray or talk to Hei and your problem goes away. That's fine, but it will probably work only according to the healing power of nature and the influence of positive thinking. Miracles, like a statue crying blood, are only trying to bring hope to the gullible and credulous. Even if you believed that it was real, there is no reason to believe in a God that interferes in your life.

What puzzles skeptics is not so much that miracles might occur, but that God, the same deity who created the world in six days and parted the Red Sea, would mess around with trivial stuff like weeping statues. To them, the oft-invoked notion that God works in mysterious ways is just shorthand for P.T. Barnum's maxim: 'There's a sucker born every minute.'

People have prayed for their wart to disappear, and sometime later, when it did, they say, 'See what prayer can do.' But they don't think about the many more who prayed whose warts didn't go, or the large number who didn't pray whose warts did disappear. (Many now know that warts can be made gradually to disappear by licking them frequently or by wetting with dilute acid frequently.)

Why should religion be involved with how we live? If you want to pour out your problems and worries to God, that's probably good. Psychologists tell us that it helps you to clarify and analyze the problem, so you can better see how to proceed. But why should you let the so-called religious writings, such as the bible, dictate your refusal to eat pork or govern whom you should enjoy sex with?

If the bible was God's commandment of how to live, Ee should have included some far more important don'ts, such as not eating animal fat. Use religion to think about an after-life, if you want one, but don't use the bible, written by men long ago, to guide you in your daily problems. Our present human brain can do a much better job.

You are asked to believe that God communicated with the prophets to say what was right or wrong for humans for all time, and if this came from God it must be right. Well, it does not make sense when you realize that what each heard was influenced by that prophet's environment which was so different from today's over-population. You should much prefer to listen to the psychologists, sociologists, writers, speakers and teachers of the present generation to find the best moral and ethical way to live in today's environment.

We need a global code of ethics produced from a scientific philosophy, not from a voodoo-type wizard called God. If you don't believe in your prophet because of all the inconsistencies, how can you believe him about God, soul, after-life, etc. It is much more satisfying if you find a belief, such as the Unified Life Theory, which is logical, rational, reasonable, predictable, based on scientific knowledge and gives a basis for obtaining answers to all your questions about how life should be lived. Life is real and earnest and not a charming fairy tale.

The Unified Life Theory frees you from 'sin' because there is no such thing as sin. Religious people believe that sin is doing something or even thinking something that is contrary to God's laws. But there are no 'God's laws'. People do things because at the time it seems the best thing for them to do, or because they instinctively reacted to a situation. Animals don't sin. They do what is necessary to stay alive.

If you are sorry for something you have done, and you wish you hadn't done it, you should not want a God to forgive, so you can forget. You should use the memory of your action to help remember not to do the same again.

The Unified Life Theory says that humans are animals, and that God, if there is one, does not interfere with the laws of nature. The Unified Life Theory is logical, straightforward and easy to relate to.

We don't know how the universe began. We assume the 'big bang', but don't know what was there before. Just because we don't know, it doesn't mean we have to make up a story. It would be interesting to know, but we probably never will, and it doesn't make much difference. We should get on with our lives, and try to make this living experience as enjoyable as possible. Heaven on earth is having a goal; striving for a goal; reaching; looking back and saying 'I did it'; and helping others find their goal.

There is no God to help you. You've got to help yourself. Your desire for love and affection should be re-directed to loving yourself. 'I love me' and 'I like me' should be your mottos. Learn to love yourself. No one else will love you to your satisfaction. You are sure to be disappointed if you rely on a God, another human or a pet for that love and affection you need. We should come out of the closet and have some revival meetings to proclaim our faith in ourselves.

The only religion you need is faith in logic and science, or as Einstein said, 'To me it is enough to wonder at the secretes.'

THE PURPOSE IN LIFE IS HAPPINESS

We laugh, we cry, we are born, we die,
Who will riddle me the how and why?
Alfred, Lord Tennyson

Religious people feel there is a purpose in life, or a meaning to life, but can't explain what it is. Ministers say we are to serve God so we can live in eternity with God. If God wanted so much company up there Ee shouldn't have put us through so much trouble to get us there.

What does Ee want us to do to serve Hei except be good? But that does not appeal to many of us as a real purpose for us to go through all this earthly misery. What would be a 'good life'? What would be best? Is there a goal? Why are we here?

There is no hard evidence of a purpose in any life, including ours. If there is none, then what? We can't imagine that other animals have brains that would ask the same question, but just because we do ask the question doesn't mean that there is a satisfactory answer.

The Unified Life Theory suggests that the only goal is to get through life with as little pain, stress and suffering as possible, and as much of the good life as possible. The good life includes contentment, excitement, satisfaction, happiness and pleasure. Searching for pleasure and avoiding pain is not what we should do, so much as it is what we do. However, each person has ee's own view as to what pleasure is.

This may sound like the 'me generation', but that is not bad for humans if they realize that the only way to have the good life is to live in a society which makes it possible. This means that people will work toward having the good life for themselves, but at the same time will not do things that would take away from other people's happiness or good life. 'Your rights end where your neighbour's nose begins.'

This is based on the ten commandments. Do to others what you would have them do to you, and don't do to others what you would not want them to do to you. People are giving and helpful, because they want to create a society that would do the same for them.

Morals must become what our society feels is best, but that does not mean that all people will have the same moral code. We should strive for a society where each individual is able to get as much pleasure out of life in ee's own way as long as this does not interfere too greatly with another's pleasure.

In many cases a person will suffer great hardship and pain, like going into a burning building to rescue a child. Ee does it because the result will give hei pleasure. All our actions are based on the pleasure it gives us. Take any of the actions where people might say, 'Why would they go through that when there is so much hard work, pain or suffering?'

The reason is that not to do it would cause greater mental pain. They could not be happy knowing what would happen if they didn't do it. These people do what they have to do so they won't hate themselves afterward for not trying. A brave nam has done something that is dangerous to do. A hero has done something that is not only dangerous but seems impossible to do. 'You're a better man than I am, Gunga Din.'

Is there such a thing as a genetically programmed purpose in life? Let's take a look at our mammalian ancestors, because it would seem that they did have a definite purpose in life. The only breed of mammals that survived over millions of years were the ones where the males were genetically programmed to have only one purpose in life, and that was to have intercourse and ejaculate into a female.

They also had to be programmed to be successful at finding food and staying alive, but their only aim in life was to have a harem or at least have access to many females. This was their symbol of success, and it decided their standing in their society. They fought anyone who challenged their rating, and if any other male tried to steal, coax away, or mount one of their females, they immediately went into a rage and attacked the intruder.

Humans survived, because they have the same genetic programming. We still have the same drive today, and our society has not tried to analyze the reason for this feeling. People just go along promoting sex, romance and a relationship as the supreme achievement, the most rewarding, the most honourable and the most noble purpose in life. Our communication media spend most of their time discussing or picturing the soap operas of life, and 90% of the songs sung are about romance or the lack of it.

A man boasts about his wife and children, and in our society's eyes that makes him the super man. All a man needs to do, to establish a high standing in the community, is to show that he has assumed his obligation by being responsible for a wife and children. It's not known whether he beats his wife and kids or not. It is sufficient that he is a husband and father.

You can see how powerful the programming is, both from our genes and the communications environment, but this is not the best system for this present society. You can understand some of the bad results when you see the number of men who are driven to do what their ancestors did, namely, harm their wives or girlfriends who try to leave them or are found to be unfaithful to them. They batter and bash them about, and in some cases they even kill.

We should not be surprised. They are doing what they were programmed to do. It is only by education and using our brains that we can overcome this programming which was necessary for survival only a few generations back.

If our brains were to analyze how our society has changed from the wild animal beginnings, we would see that brains and mouths have developed language, and hands have developed so many activities where we can be achievers. These pleasures and goals have become far more important than the desire for romance and children.

We enjoy doing something that we are good at, or that gives us pleasure, when we think we can achieve some proficiency. If your brain were to stop and analyze what gives you the most pleasure, most of you will not find it in your marriage and children. Sure, some do, but any honest survey would show that climbing your mountains or achieving special goals are far more important and enjoyable than the pleasures of the nuclear family.

Our purpose in life is to avoid pain and find pleasure. We must use our brains to realize that our programming for romance may have been best in the past, but is not true now. We should stop thinking that we must find a mate, because that is not where we will find the most happiness. Spend your time on more enjoyable pursuits. Sure, if romance comes, enjoy it if you can, and while you can, but don't grieve if you don't. It leads to a lot of frustration, pain and suffering.

What is the best way, both physically and socially, for humans to live a more enjoyable life? Life is a game, a very tough game that we all have to play. The game goes on all the time and never stops. Life is not fair. Good things happen to bad people, and bad things happen to good people.

Some of us are winners almost all the time; some win only sometimes; and some never win. It is an ill-conceived world, but we all keep trying to get some pleasure out of it.

Life is like a box of chocolates. You never know what you are going to get. Life is a journey and also a conundrum. It is full of horrible pain and suffering, and sometimes full of a certain amount of joy and pleasure. The mix is different for everyone. Some have more pain than others, not because they deserve it, but because that's the way it happened. It was this way back in the stone age and before.

It was and still is the same for all animals. Most animals live with fear of the predator, and the greatest pain is being eaten slowly, piece by piece while still conscious. Sickness and injury are painful. Mosquito, fly and parasite bites are painful to all animals, including humans.

If life was so awful, why did not the animals, including humans, kill themselves? Because any strain of living beings that did so would be eliminated from the gene pool, so we assume that the animal strains that survived were genetically programmed to want to stay alive. Therefore, the programming for our ancestors must have been very strong to survive, because life had so much pain and suffering. Today in the developed countries, life is much better in some ways. We are less often sick; we have pain-killers;

we have appliances and labour-saving devices; and we have a social system that gives us a high standard of living.

If nam's purpose is to enjoy life as much as possible, then it is interesting to note that each of us finds enjoyment in our own individual way. Some activities are physical and others mental. What is enjoyed by one is not enjoyed by another. The things we enjoy doing most are activities that we do well, not necessarily better than anyone else, but maybe better than most.

You can be happy that you are better than the average in your group, even though your group is not the upper half of all the groups in your town or county or country. You might even be happy to just be in your group, even though you are the lowest ranking in the group. To reach the goal of being best at something, at some level, is a most satisfying goal. Trying to be the best we can be sometimes takes a lot of hard work, but the trying is worthwhile no matter what level we reach.

The human animal today cannot live like ee's ancestors. Ee no longer can be a hunter, gatherer, eat the animals ee kills or even grow all ee's own food. Ee can't get water from a nearby stream or build ee's own shelter from materials of the forest. Ee is born into a society where ee must spend years studying and learning, and then work at a job to get money to buy the food and water and housing supplied by the efforts of others.

Does the Unified Life Theory tell us what to do? Not really, but it does recommend the goals of happiness, contentment, pleasure, the feeling of achievement, etc. Because we are so inter-dependent we will realize that we cannot reach all these goals, or even just one, unless we work for a society which allows these goals to be reached by all. The Unified Life Theory would suggest that we should use our brains to arrive at logical decisions as to what changes should be brought about to make this a better society.

We will never know the 'why' of our universe, our world, our life. To think of it as 'happenstance' is not bad. Things have progressed in a logical fashion with actions always being repeated in the same way, so that we have been able to define them as 'laws of nature'. Volcanoes erupt and then die out; trees sprout up and eventually die; insects, animals, and people live and die; eventually our sun will die and with it all living things on our earth.

After only a few thousand years we humans have become so populous that we are already making an impact on our environment by farming, cutting, digging and building. We are on the edge of disaster, what with garbage, water, carbon dioxide, ozone, atomic waste, AIDS, etc. Too many think we are God's chosen people, and that Ee will help us overcome our problems. Well, Ee won't save the human animal any more than Ee saved the dinosaurs who were masters of their environment for 150 million years.

Scientists expect that something will happen before too long that will kill off all the humans. It could be an influenza virus that has mutated until it is resistant to mankind's most potent drugs, or a large meteor impact. There is no God to save us. Can you see any 'purpose in life' in all this?

Someone made the observation, 'I've been sentenced to life on earth without even being told what the charges were.' So we might as well just make the most of it. Just laugh and say, 'That's the way the ball bounces.' Laughter in the face of reality is the finest sound in the universe. 'What we're meant to do, I hope, is to fill some small and temporary slot, to give off a little light for a little while and then lie down.' Life is a terminal illness, but we don't know how or when. How about some palliative care?

Did you know that senior citizens are the nations' leading carriers of AIDS:

Hearing AIDS
Band AIDS
Walking AIDS
Government AIDS
Medical AIDS
Monetary AIDS (to their kids).

MARRIAGE IS NOT THE BEST

One third of modern nam's time is spent sleeping, one third working and one third in the 'married' environment. Is the married environment conducive to the Unified Life Theory's goal to avoid pain and suffering and to find as much joy, happiness and contentment as possible? It too often is not. If it is not, what would be better? Let's take a look.

Back in the stone age our ancestors were not monogamous. Only the dominant male was allowed to serve his harem in his territory, and other males did without or established their harems in other areas. Pair-bonding in the animal kingdom was not common.

When reproduction was understood, the idea of owning property was established. Farming became the major activity, and as each man came to own his portion of land, it became customary for him to have a small harem. However, as the population of males and females was almost even, it soon became customary for a male to have one woman, the pair-bond. He owned the property and the woman and children, and the man was dominant in all respects, and thus the nuclear family was established. Religion made the pair-bond official. It was called 'marriage'. It is assumed that human pair-bonding is not a genetic thing, but a social development for the conditions that existed back then.

This lasted until after World Wars One and Two, when women entered the work-force and began having fewer babies. This brought about a big change in the meaning of marriage, even to the extent that in North America, marriage, by law, means sharing resources equally. So what can we now expect marriage to be like?

Before World War Two, a man was socialized to be strong, active and powerful, a woman to be passive and nurturing, to be good, a good daughter, a good friend, a good date, a good guest and good in bed. A married woman played the role of enabler, helping everyone else.

Marriage was God's plan for nem. If you didn't get married you were going against God's will. A girl was brought up on the assumption that she would get married, have children and be a housewife, giving care and comfort to her husband and children. She changed her name to her husband's, which implied that he was dominant, and that she was giving herself to him. There was a sort of barrel marked 'his', and all the women and children put all their energies into that big barrel.

She was to measure her success in life by how 'good' and successful a man she was able to marry, how 'good' a wife and mother she was, and how successful her children became. In other words, motherhood was not expected to get her into the history books.

Women were restricted to giving birth and maintaining homes under the proliferating and ever-stricter rules and manners of Victorian society. Lack of birth-control and education, bound working-class women to raising the children needed as workers for the factories or fodder for the battle-fields. Because money became most important, value was attributed to paid work only. Women's work, unseen except in the home, was devalued because it earned no money. Women were taught few skills, and they and their children were entirely dependent on men for money and security.

A boy's lot in life was to get an education, get a good job, make money, get married, have children and live in a nice home. Having children was what life was all about. He was to measure his success in life by his success in his job, by the beauty and charm of the woman he married, by the size of his home, and by the success of his children.

There was no thought of discussing whether this was the best way to live. This was the way it was. When a man got married, his wife stopped working. He was to be the provider and had to be seen as the provider. Almost every social activity was based on couples. There was practically no place for a bachelor. Getting married was a must.

In the first half of the twentieth century, boys were brought up to think of girls as the weaker sex who must be protected. Boys were to treat girls as if they were delicate china to be handled gently, to be saved from having to do heavy physical work, to be given the best seat, the best food, the best of everything.

Many boys felt that passionate kissing (with a girl who would be the type he would want to marry) would be tantamount to a proposal of marriage. But some girls were different, and if a fellow somehow assumed that she was not likely to be among those he would look to for marriage, then he would be able to have many car sessions, heavy petting above the waist and wonderful kisses.

He would never consider intercourse, although he surely would want to. He knew others were doing it, because of the condoms around the parking spots. He would be afraid of a pregnancy, and he felt intercourse should be with the girl he married. He would feel that being married to a smart girl would make him feel inferior. He would probably marry a girl he thought would make an excellent mother.

Getting married was a must for a woman who wanted children and family. She needed to 'get a man' to support the family, to be the protector, the handy-man. In many cases she married the first man who asked her. She was afraid she might not get another proposal. Having children, a family and a home was far more important than her relationship with the man. Besides, raising children without a man was not considered a rational option.

Many women today are satisfied to be at home with their children. They are the lucky few who have husbands who are good to them and are happy with the arrangement. But statistics show that 'good' men are getting fewer every year. Too often 'mister right' doesn't turn out to be the right man after marriage.

After the children come, he loses his job and can't find another; he runs off with her money; he doesn't give her enough money, even though he has lots, and criticizes her for not being a careful shopper; he drinks or gambles away most of the money; he turns out to be a child molester of his own children, just like the lions who eat the cubs; he turns out to be a wife-beater, just like the male baboon who crushes the skull of the female for exhibiting the slightest hint of insubordination. And still women will get married to have children, even knowing the risks. It is difficult to understand why.

There have been many good, happy and satisfying marriages, but those have been mostly where one of the couple was indisputably dominant, a benevolent despot, and the partner was happy with the arrangement. Also, when society is so rigidly structured, and the way of life is strict and preset, then marriage of any two people, even if pre-arranged by parents, would possibly be considered good.

A man would feel that marriage is wonderful if he has a wife who thinks he is wonderful; who is good in bed; a good cook; spends a lot of time doing wonderful wifely things; is cheerful and happy; runs the house and brings up the children the way he wants.

Many a married woman is happy when her husband spends enough money on her and treats her like a princess. If she feels her husband's requests, beliefs and decisions are the best, and if her desired way of life is the same as his, all is well. Society looks upon them as pillars of society, and arranges the tax forms to reduce the taxes of married couples.

Marriage is good when there is a state of mutual trust, love, cooperation, forgiveness, tenderness, unselfishness, kindness, and generosity of heart. To know that you have someone who will stick by and help you through a sickness or a tragedy is most wonderful. Unfortunately, the possibility of two people of this compatibility getting together is small, but people will still get married, hoping that they will be lucky. If they get divorced, they will still try and try again, because they think marriage is the only possible way to have a happy life.

Obviously the bad marriages are ones where the compatibility is not there. As a matter of interest, here are some examples of conflicting desires. He doesn't want to tip the waitree; she insists / he wants a trailer; she wants a cottage / he wants a green wagon; she wants a blue sedan / he wants to bring up the children to be familiar and unconcerned with seeing the unclothed body; she insists that occurs only while dressing, if at all / he wants to be a nudist; she refuses / she likes dinner late; he likes it early / he wants a moustache and beard; she hates it / he wants more sex; she wants less / he wants more cuddling and touching; she only wants to cry on his shoulder. He was born in bed with a naked woman and hopes to exit the same way. Why can't a woman be more like a man?

Skip the next long paragraph if you are already remembering your own many experiences, and feel you don't need to dwell on the other horror stories. If you are not married, or not living with someone, you should read on so you can chuckle at the many problems you won't need to face. It's pretty meaty stuff, so keep a napkin handy.

He wants to live frugally and do without in order to save for the future and retirement; she insists on maintaining a standard of living consistent with their position in society as governed by the job he holds / he can enjoy many sports; she none / she wants both to sleep in the same bed, because 'couples who sleep together, stay together'; he can't get to sleep with her reading in bed / she likes parties; he doesn't / she has her bottles and paraphernalia all over the bathroom counter and shelves; there is no room for his / she says he must wash his hands before a meal; he says washing hands is no more effective than wringing them / he tips his soup bowl in; she wants him to tip his soup bowl out / he wants to drive to get there; she wants to go slowly and view the scenery / he uses his fork to cut most foods; she wants him to always use his knife, and abide by all the 'proper' table manners / he wants short hair; she wants his long / he says a dirty shirt or sheets are just as comfortable as clean ones; she says they are unaesthetic and unsanitary / she says if he loved her he would do these things to make her happy; he says if she loved him she would not ask him to change.

You might start out in marriage with a knight in shining armour and be relatively compatible. You assume this will continue, but almost certainly it won't, especially if the man is the only breadwinner. Big differences are going to develop because of your different environments, he in the work-place, and you at home with the children. Your desires and expectations change dramatically. Some changes can be minor, like one wanting to be a nudist, but other changes can be devastating, such as him starting to rob banks, to bash you about or assault the children.

You really never know what you've got. When a woman is thinking of getting married, it is important that she know if her intended already has a wife, or a string of girl-friends and abandoned children; if he is in debt; if he has a good enough job; if he is of good character, or a deadbeat. Many hire private eyes, at great expense, to check them out. However, if she is not intending to get herself tied up, none of these things are of great importance. She can enjoy the company of many, for various activities, without knowing their personal history.

Some people love pets, even though they know that they will have to spend a great deal of time walking, feeding, cleaning up after, scolding, training, medicating, spending money on, and searching for the pet. They feel they are rewarded sufficiently, but mainly it is a job they are dedicated to. Marriage is like that, but remember, pets don't change very much.

You say sex should not be just a physical act, but a chance to show love and affection, and a time to tell the other of your admiration and thankfulness for all the nice things ee has done. It should be, and it is so nice when it happens, but in most cases each cannot forget the things the other didn't do: you wouldn't buy the cottage, you bought the trailer instead; you won't give me what I want, so you won't get what you want; you were so critical; I resent your constant long business trips.

It's difficult to feel that romantic love, so it mostly comes down to trying to help the other enjoy the physical part. Some say sex with their wives becomes more like sex with an ice cube with a hole in it.

When trying to decide whether to get married or not, a man should consider that his wife will be his favourite charity that will use up approximately 95% of his salary. The function of that charity is to give food, clothing and comfort to the husband, children, grandmother, church, women's aid, relatives and neighbours, and for the wife to be able to do her thing. After some years, if the husband should suggest that he is not receiving much in the way of comfort and also would like to start doing his thing, she has been known to leave and, according to the law, take half his property and accept support for the rest of her life, thereby cutting him off from all benefits. A man should be most careful in deciding what charity to support.

He should know what Mr. Bumble (in *Oliver Twist*, by Charles

Dickens) said about husbands being responsible for their wives: 'The law is an ass.'

When a man gets married he thinks he is getting a woman who thinks he is quite wonderful. All his younger life he has found that to be praised produced a wonderful feeling. Most of this would come from his parents and teachers who make a point of giving praise where possible, because it is so good for the child. However, little is received from his peers, so when he gets this from a girl, it's a marvellous feeling.

Unfortunately, once married, if the wife becomes unhappy with something he does, he gets little praise from her. How can she tell him he is wonderful when he is not? How can she put her arms around him and say, 'I love you' when she doesn't. Marriage for a man (or woman) is to have someone who will stick by you through thick and thin, and give you the support you so badly want, but most often you don't get it. Behind every successful man stands a surprised woman.

What a man wants is unconditional love. No matter how much anxiety he causes, he wants her to forgive and greet him joyfully the next morning. Not many women can do that. So, don't get married.

If you are looking for that one and only you can spend the rest of your life with, you are looking for someone to tell you how wonderful and worthwhile you are. Each individual should be happy with <u>heiself</u>. <u>Ee</u> knows <u>ee</u> is not smartest or best, but <u>ee</u> should learn to take pride in the things <u>ee</u> does do well. If you yearn for praise from others, you will always be disappointed. Keep saying, 'I like me. I'm special because I'm me.'

For some people the approval of others becomes an obsession. For such people, affection is not enough; appreciation is not enough; they must be adored constantly. They must hear somebody promise love and honour forever. Frequently it takes several somebodies, because those hooked on applause can never get enough.

Even in the 1950s the 'good' husbands made their wives feel that the marriage was a partnership, but in many cases the housewife was able to take control. If the house was put in both names, when the house was sold the wife could take her half of the money and do what she wanted with it. In other words the husband lost control of the money. Not many men want their wives to control the money that they make, especially if they are making a good salary.

To the man, the partnership means that he is quite happy to have his wife share in his standard of living, but he does not want his wife to spend his money on things he does not approve. The wife may think she is entitled to half his salary, but the husband probably won't think so, especially if he feels she is not that good a cook, or not that good a wife and mother. His worth is measured by his salary, and if it is a good one, he doesn't feel his wife's work is worth very much in comparison.

If they both agree to try to make it fifty-fifty partnership, they have problems. The wedding ceremony often says something to the effect that the bride and groom 'are now become as one'. That's like having a body with two heads, which would never work. Each will feel that the other is spending or controlling more than ee's share of the money. You buy something and the other thinks you are getting more than your share. You can't really buy your spouse an expensive present for fear ee will think it is half their money poorly spent. Fifty-fifty means that you both have to give up doing what annoys the other, and one will always think ee is giving up much more. It's like agreeing to live with only 50% of your desires, and that's not a happy life.

Business consultants tell us that fifty-fifty partnerships are discouraged 90% of the time, because so many fall apart, just like the Mitchells and McCain food family. Often one partner is the inventor and manufacturer and the other is the financier and salesnam. One will always feel that ee is contributing so much more or ee doesn't like what the other is doing, and since neither has a majority vote or control, nothing is done and the partnership flounders. The same is true of a fifty-fifty marriage. No-one has the final say. One yes and one no means no solution until someone backs down. This is living at a 50% level of happiness, so therefore marriage is not the best social arrangement for humans.

Many wives feel that if they have to get a divorce they will get half their husband's salary and half of everything else, but in many cases the wife doesn't get very much. Most men, who have been happy to share their income with their stay-at-home wives, have, in most cases, no desire to pay anything if the wife has left. Paying and getting nothing in return would be unreasonable. Sometimes the husband disappears, is now unemployed, or just doesn't pay up. If the wife has no money-making skills, she and the children go on welfare, and she hopes she can find another man. Unfortunately, because men die years earlier than women, she will likely be left on her own, with little income.

Marlo Thomas said, 'Marriage is like a vacuum cleaner. You stick it to your ear and shhlllurrrppp, it sucks out all your energy and ambition.' In North America, 90% of families are dysfunctional.

The problems arise when one promises to love, cherish, and be faithful for always, and then isn't or doesn't. When that happens the other feels cheated, feels betrayed, feels devastated, feels ee wants to hit out and punish. Males want sexual access to women, but cannot bear it when other men have access to their mates. Therefore, it is best not to make commitments. No commitment, no promise, means less danger of men attacking women. Friends can drift apart. Marrieds can't.

Why do we think marriage is the only possible way, when we know that everyone is not equipped to be a good partner or parent? Why do we assume that marriage and family life are the main purpose of human existence? Why do so many proclaim to be happily married, when we know that only about one in twenty marriages is worth trying to save? Yet, society's tacit assumption is that all normal people are qualified for marriage, and this is not so.

It's a tough job, and most people fail at it. Wedlock is a term that implies being locked in. When sexual attraction is the main reason for marriage, the consequences are often unfortunate. Of all the decisions we make in our lives, marriage is the biggest and riskiest and least reversible, especially if you have children. If wedlock doesn't bring happiness, having children certainly won't.

When both partners are wage-earners, many women will still want to get married for security, to have a strong male around the house, to do the heavy work and to be a companion. Men will be getting married for prestige, for a regular sex partner and for the couple situation. However, he will probably not get the regular cook and housewife.

They may both be getting married to have children, but this will be a problem if they both continue to work. In so many cases the pre-school children will be cared for during the day by new immigrants, and school-age children will become latch-key kids. Both are poor arrangements. In any case, if they try to have a fifty-fifty marriage, they will be faced with all the problems of a partnership, and their chances of success are small. Marriage is like Russian roulette with half the chambers loaded. Your chances of being clobbered are great.

All young men were told by their parents to 'grow up and take your responsibility.' This meant get a job, get married and have children. It is your duty. Only in this way can you fulfil your debt to society for having brought you this far. In the past this was necessary to keep the population growing so that humans could fulfil the purpose in life that God had for humans. No doubt people felt that to be married was the proper and blissful state.

You may say that only in a nuclear family will you have the dedication of sons and daughters to take care of old and feeble or sick parents, and the dedication of brothers and sisters for each other. The examples of selflessness for a relative are legion, but more and more there are growing numbers of old people neglected by their children.

Our society has always stressed the marriage commitment and responsibility to try to protect women and children, but this has failed in so many ways, resulting in wife beatings, child abuse, and sex abuse.

Commitment and responsibility to spouse, children and parents can be quite wonderful, but for many it has not brought the happiness or pleasure envisioned. Other than being a pleasure to help others, it turns out to be a job, a lot of work that is not often rewarding. Responsibility is 'a duty', a must-do obligation, a burden, a real misery, an action imposed by society, a restriction. Once you 'take responsibility' you are no longer free.

Responsibility usually entails time, effort and money. Don't spend it unless the rewards are worth it. You should only be responsible for getting as good an education as you can master, getting good exercise and food for your body and getting a satisfactory job. Don't take on the responsibility for another person unless it is a paying job you can enjoy, such as being a teacher or care-person.

When a man is married, he can't take the risks or do some of the things he would like to do because he can't subject his wife to the problems of going broke or whatever. Having a wife is like having a child. Even if she does not show affection or think you are very wonderful, or if you don't really like what she does, you still are expected to love her, because that is the responsibility which society demands.

A man should consider the marriage vows, which to some extent define responsibility, such as 'to love, honour and obey, in sickness and in health, for better or worse, for richer or poorer, until death us do part.' A man might then decide not to put himself in a position in which he cannot seek enjoyment elsewhere if his wife turns out not to be good at making sex enjoyable and is not often willing. Ee shouldn't get oneself locked into something in such a way that later, if ee finds ee doesn't like it ee can't get out without affecting other lives so drastically.

Our society should not try to insist that a woman takes care of a hypochondriac who doesn't even try to keep a job, and browbeats her at every turn. A woman should not have to give a man the sexual intercourse he so desires when she knows she won't enjoy it. There are some women who feel that intercourse should be for one purpose, to try to make babies. It is interesting to note that no other animal seems to think that sex is to create offspring.

Marriage is not the best for the majority. This is clearly indicated by the fact that Ottawa's Vanier Institute of the Family expects that 40% of marriages performed today will end in separation or divorce. Studies show that the percentage of households occupied by married couples with children has dropped to 25%, and a large number of families are headed by single or divorced mothers living below the poverty line.

We have to agree that just because the bible and other religious writings talk of marriage as being a holy state, required by God, does not make it so. Nothing is holy or sacred if there is no God. Marriage is not an institution decreed by laws chiselled in stone.

Common-law unions are really not much better. They last for a shorter time even than marriages, on average about five years. Neither can be good for children. Marriage will probably gradually disappear and become as uncommon as harems and bigamy are today.

Our present day sociologists are far better at analyzing what is best for the twenty-first century than the religious prophets of 2000 years ago. We have to agree that a marriage ceremony does not make two people 'as one'. And even if couples sleep together, they won't necessarily stay together. Each has distinctive fingerprints, and genes unlike anyone else, and they can only be truly happy if they can be themselves. They cannot be themselves if they dedicate themselves to another for the rest of their lives. This kind of commitment and responsibility is a trap that too often is not enjoyable.

What should a couple do if they are desperately in love? They should arrange to be with each other as much as they desire or can, but they should not propose marriage to prove to the other that they want to commit themselves to the other for ever and ever.

You may feel that you want to make the commitment, but don't listen to your heart; listen to your brain, and that should tell you that the romantic feeling will not last. You will both change, and even if you both want to raise children, you should consider the following chapter, *A Sofraternity is Better*. Some say marriage is too often an institution that gives children a false sense of security. The nuclear family would soon disappear if it were agreed that a woman should have only one child in order to control population, because a single child situation is not ideal or even good for the child or parent.

Most parents still tell their children that marriage is the best arrangement, even if their own marriage was not. Even if they are separated or divorced they would feel that it was their fault that their marriage did not turn out to be a blissful wonderful life, and would proclaim marriage as the ideal.

They do this because they do not wish to admit that the choice made by them, their parents, God and all their ancestors, was not the best. They can't believe that their whole philosophy of life was wrong. They believed that almost all other marriages were good, but we now know that all those friends, acquaintances and relatives that we thought were happy were not so happy after all. Marriage is as out-dated as our calendar. It is something we grew up with. It isn't logical and it isn't the best arrangement.

A nam owes it to heiself to stop and consider the advantages of the single life. Think about it. There is no substitute for freedom. You can, if you wish, find a cheap place to live. Who needs a mansion? You put your money in the bank, and you furnish your place as you please. You come and go as it pleases you. Enjoy yourself. That's what we're here for.

'The golden age of family bliss exists more in people's imagination than in their experience.'

'Marriage for a woman is like a brassière. She would like to get rid of it, but she needs the support.'

'He promised me a rose garden, but I don't like the thorns I have now.'

'Life is lonesome, but lonesome isn't bad.'

'Monogamy sounds like monotony.'

'She looks desirable, but her valley of temptation is all dried up.'

'As the British would say, "No sex please, we're married".'

'Marriage is the only war where you sleep with the enemy.'

'He wonders if the fucking he gets is worth the fucking he gets.'

A SOFRATERNITY IS BETTER

The alternative to marriage is not married – single. You can have everything you can get in a marriage without promising to be a good husband or wife forever and ever, come 'hell or high water'. There is no 'mister right', 'the right one', 'one and only love', that you should marry and live with for the rest of your life. If there were, he would be on the other side of the world, and you would never meet him. You don't have to be married to have love and affection.

You don't have to be married to be in a relationship. You don't have to be married to be a member of a family. You can be a member of an extended family, such as your lodge, your housing group or your tennis group, etc. The happiest, most sensible way to live, is not within the lonely confines of the nuclear family, but in the expansive embrace of the extended family. You can give your complete loyalty to your extended family, and women don't even have to change their names. It has always been true that many family members find people outside the family who are closer to them than their own family, so extended family is normal.

It is almost certain that early hunters and gatherers did not have the bond between mother, father and children that we expect today. Primitive people rarely expected continuous companionship between parents or between father and young children. The idea of the perpetually loving and responsible father of young children is probably the most artificial creation of human society, and the farthest from our natural instinct.

Future generations will find that marriage and the nuclear family are not the best. To live alone in a house or apartment is not good because it is difficult to find people with the same likes, and too often friends are not nearby. The preferred arrangement would be to be a member of an extended family. This could be like a college fraternity or sorority, only larger and co-ed, and part of a national group, with 'sofraternities' in all major centres.

Just like there are many differently named fraternities at each college or university, there would be many sofraternities with different names. However, a sofraternity of one name would be similar throughout all locations. Each named sofraternity would have distinctive features, goals and aims, probably based on activities. Some might be based on one's working occupation: farming, engineering, civil service, children-raising, etc. Some might be based on one's leisure activities: tennis, golf, bridge, etc. and probably combinations. Each named sofraternity would have the same activity emphasis, and be your extended family.

Your immediate family would be the people in your own 'house'. Each named sofraternity would have a common external identifying feature. Some might have a large amount of one or two storey accommodation for people who want to be able to walk out of the door to a back-yard. Some might be like existing condominiums.

A unique architectural design would be a complex consisting of four condominiums or apartments, one on each side of a large square, with three tennis courts in the middle. The main feature of this arrangement is to avoid having underground parking and enclosed elevators where people are so often attacked. Instead, this arrangement would have a space to park your car right at your back door. This parking arrangement is safer and more convenient than parking your car in a private home drive-way. It would be almost impossible for a thief or attacker to be hiding when you drove up. The car elevators are also to be used by pedestrian members, and, being open, there is no place for attackers to hide. There is no separate, possibly dangerous, passenger elevator.

The passing lane is one-way, and, because the car elevators are at the diagonal corners, you do not have far to go. If one elevator is down for repairs, you can drive around and use the other. To be more luxurious you could have an elevator at each corner.

Whether you are walking or in a car, your identity card is used to bring the elevator. There is no lobby, and mail-boxes are at ground level, beside the elevators.

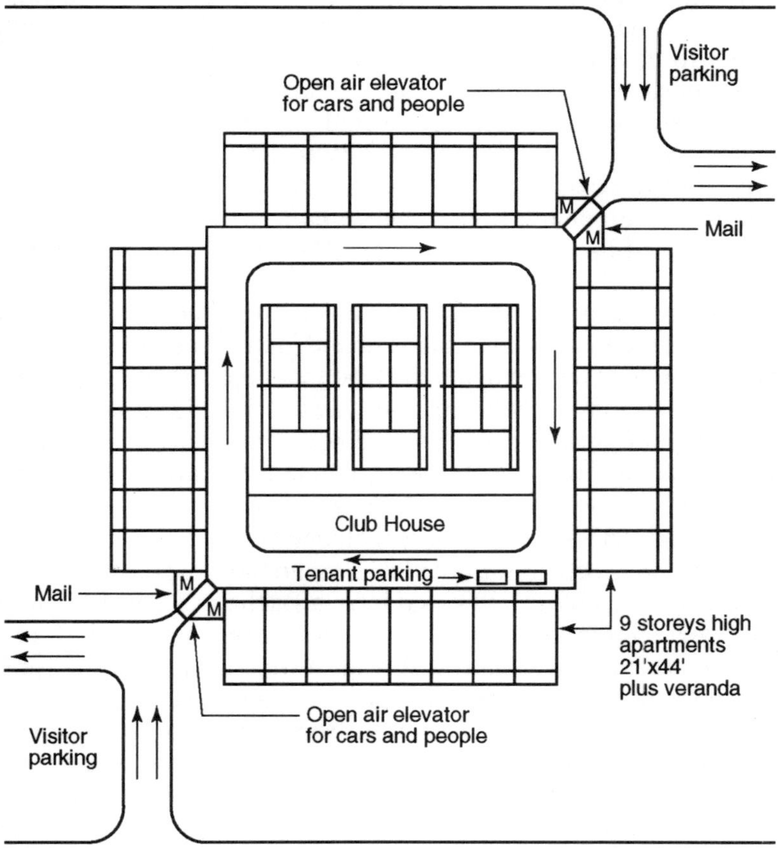
Visitor parking
Open air elevator for cars and people
M
M
Mail
Club House
Tenant parking
Mail
M
M
9 storeys high apartments 21'x44' plus veranda
Visitor parking
Open air elevator for cars and people

Sofraternities would have English alphabet letters rather than Greek letters, and the letters would stand for the activities predominating. A tennis-playing, bridge-playing, nudist could be a member of the TBN family and have a condo in a TBN house. Some sofraternities would be large enough to have a restaurant in the building, and the club-house could have equipment for bridge, ping-pong, darts, etc. Each might have a few apartments available to rent to travellers or vacationers who were members of another TBN house, your extended family.

Members of a sofraternity would be expected to help one another. Some would be born and raised there. Others would have to be sponsored by a member and be voted in by a large majority. One reason a person might want to be a member would be the reputation of that sofraternity for being a warm, loving, helping family.

With an extended family, you are more likely to find more happiness than you might have received in the nuclear family. You can find friends and companions who you think are quite wonderful and who think you are quite wonderful. They will likely become your good friends. You are not so intimately tied to each other. They are not so often disappointed, because they are not expecting as much from you as if you were married.

You are interacting with more than one person on a level, and in activities, that you both can enjoy. You are not responsible for all the others' activities. You could have a Bachelor's and Spinster's Ball where no-one is trying to snare another into marriage.

In the sofraternity some will want their own apartment; some will have their own apartment adjoining their best friend's apartment, with adjoining doors maybe; some will share their apartment with another, but it would be expected that you would have more than one friend. If friendships sour, don't get mad, change your apartment.

In Sweden lifestyles have changed already. Marriage is not the norm. Half of all births are out of wedlock, and most Stockholm residents live alone. Some singles today are lonely, because our society is not yet geared to this lifestyle. When singles are far more numerous, and when we have more sofraternities established, then life will be better. Many will want the advantages of living alone: you don't have to keep closing and opening the bathroom door; you can eat when you want, what you want, and you can leave things lying around where they are handy, etc.

Love is a many-splendoured thing. Sex plus admiration and compatibility are often lost in marriage when you promise to be best in all three categories and then fail to be that wonderful. In the extended family arrangement, you can have your love with many people in many activities or endeavours.

There are three different Greek words for love: *eros* (sexual love), *philos* (fondness-friendship), and *agape* (brotherly love), but marriage is supposed to have seven features:

fondness = to have affection for
affection = infatuation with a person
infatuation = all-absorbing passion
passion = strong love and sexual desire
love = devotion
devotion = dedication
dedication = whole-hearted and earnest devotion.

We feel that we should take care of our old parents, because our society says we must, but it shouldn't be that way. Parents today are responsible for their children's crimes. That should make prospective parents think twice. People need and should have that wonderful feeling of security, knowing that people are there for you, ready to help, there to help make life enjoyable for you, but not from one person, 24 hours a day.

A father or mother shouldn't have to spend almost all their money on the kids and have so little for their own enjoyment, or have to work all day and be up all night with a sick one, or spend all their time with the family when it gets boring and frustrating playing kids' games for so long and so often. Sure, it is good for the children, but not from one person all the time.

It would be much better for a sofraternity to have professional parents and/or care-givers who would accept this responsibility as a paying job for a specific number of hours. If that is the work they like they can enjoy it, because they don't have to do it all the time. They would have time for other pleasures. Professional care-givers do a better job than all but a few parents when they have the time and the training to go along with their caring.

How often do we hear of the teacher who had faith and kept the student on the better path. How often have you heard a person say 'ee's always been like a guardian angel' and the person wasn't talking about ee's parent. How often we realize that young people reach beyond the family to form strong ties with others in their social network. Young adults are often not given the opportunities and secure home atmosphere that they need for a healthy development.

Teachers hear it all: A nine-year-old boy is beaten with a big spoon, and if that doesn't work his mother uses a piece of hose; a girl comes to school and is obviously starving, so the teacher starts feeding her every noon hour; a boy who is often absent admits he is exhausted, as he stays up at night protecting his mother from his father's drunken beatings.

How bad it is, or how good it was, is not important. The question is, would an extended family arrangement, such as a sofraternity, be better? It certainly should be if the sofraternity is set up to be a family where more than one or two are dedicated to your well-being.

If you don't take on the terrifying responsibility of spouse and children, you don't need life insurance, and therefore you can save yourself a lot of money. Even your will can be more flexible. You don't have to leave everything to your spouse. You could leave it to your sofraternity, or better, you could leave it to the government specifically to pay off your portion of the national debt. That is not a bad idea (see the chapter on *Fewer Laws and Less Government*).

By not marrying it is possible to love and be loved; to care for someone; to do nice things for others; to enjoy sex; to be naked when you want; to take a chance on a risky business or to do a dangerous thing; to be free.

Some birds mate for life, including golden eagles, loons and swans, but they don't have the daily problems that humans do. A gibbon is monogamous and goes several years without sex while the female is pregnant or breast-feeding her young, but only 3% of mammals are monogamous.

Once a month, the female baboon's ovaries release an egg. She then can be fertilized. Her vagina swells, turns bright pink and gives off a distinctive smell. She presents her hind-quarters to many males. The young baboons, like most mammals, start to get their own food as soon as they are weaned, and are independent soon afterward. It is not surprising then, that most female mammals can and do rear their young without any assistance from the father, and may never see the father again after copulation.

Humans, monkeys and apes are in a minority in the mammalian world, because the females conceal ovulation. We are the odd ones. With humans, neither the male nor the female knows when the female could be fertilized, until recently. We have sex at any time and all the time, even during pregnancy and after the female is no longer producing eggs.

In the past, it is assumed there was little monogamy because the female was so available to all males all the time. Therefore the paternity of the children was not necessarily known, or the relationship between copulation and parenthood understood. The children were probably taken care of by the community of women, while the men did the hunting for the whole tribe. The females of some bat species indiscriminately nurse all the young in the group.

Over time many arrangements were tried and discarded. Even today, tribes in the Brazilian rain-forest do not have marriage or a nuclear family relationship as part of their social structure. Everything is based on sharing. The hunters bring all of the meat back to be shared by all. A woman does not know who has fathered her child, because she shared her bed with more than one man. Polygamy is very much a part of mankind's past. In other words, humans shared everything.

Insects and animals probably do not know that intercourse often results in babies. Even it they did figure it out, they would probably have no way of telling others. They do it because they are genetically programmed to want to. We should not try to limit intercourse only for the purpose of begetting babies, as the church would have it. That is not the way it started. The desire for sex for a man is very powerful. It is a built-in genetic thing. If it were not for sex, we wouldn't be here. A man can't help himself, he just wants to.

The King, in *The King and I*, said a man wanting to have sex with many women was like a bumble bee wanting to taste the nectar from many flowers. All animals have this urge to some degree, and each group is turned on by certain signals or conditions.

Practically all female mammals are sexually available only when in heat, once a year. During this time they copulate a large number of times with as many different males as possible who have waited a whole year or more for the mating season. That can't be much fun for the males. Fortunately, human females are always available. Men need not go without, if they can find a willing female, but going without is not abnormal and should not be a problem.

Certainly, the nuclear family put a damper on the roving male, especially in the Victorian era of the 1800s. Women who have not been held back by the need of a husband's support have always been interested in sexual encounters. In most of the animal world, the female does not experience orgasm. Female monkeys seem to enjoy copulation (maybe it is more like wanting to pacify an itch) and even seek sex out when they are in heat, but in the 15 seconds it takes the male to enter, ejaculate, and withdraw, she would not have time to have orgasm. Human females have orgasms and can definitely enjoy it more, possibly because of their sensitive clitoris.

Male pleasure happens quickly and impulsively; female pleasure more slowly and with circumspection. Men suffer from premature ejaculation; women hardly ever. The usual method is to delay male orgasm while the female is affectionately stimulated.

The human male is noted for his desire to enter and proceed to orgasm rather quickly. This is a genetic programme handed down by his ancestors as seen in the primate group who enter and ejaculate quickly. This action was an advantage in order to avoid his prize being driven away by a rival. Men are, in general, more inclined to seek sexual relationships with a wide array of women. Masculinity and sexual prowess are very closely linked in terms of identity. It goes right to the heart of what it means to him to be a man.

With the woman it is predominately social. Her situation is

sharply different, because her level of commitment is incomparably higher than the male. She may become pregnant and have to decide whether to have an abortion, to have the child and give it up for adoption, or raise the child by herself. All of these situations are quite traumatic, unless she is very careful to choose to have sex with a man whom she believes will want to share child-rearing and living together.

Men choose women who are young and attractive. Women choose older men who are more likely to provide secure and resourceful companionship. However, once women had more reliable contraception methods, men were liberated from responsibility.

Men can be turned on by quite impersonal stimuli, such as nude female bodies in 'girlie' magazines, by strip shows and X-rated movies. Men patronize prostitutes or massage parlours where the social interaction is minimal. Equivalent facilities for women are incomparably fewer, mainly because women do not care to participate in these experiences. Their pleasures are more personal and are derived directly from psychological circumstances, with fewer partners. A man has a great desire to feel a woman's breast. He doesn't know why. He is genetically programmed to want to. He may think that to do so would turn the woman on, and that would turn him on.

There is no genetic reason for a human female to want to have intercourse with a human male. There is no genetic reason for her to have a strong desire or urge or to even enjoy the act, because in the past the genes that were passed on were from females who had little choice in the matter. The only requirement for a female's genes to be passed on were that she be attractive to the male and have genes that made her want to nurture and take care of the children, so that they survived to pass on the submissive genes.

However, women today, in their effort to be emancipated, try to have all the advantages men have, the vote, equal pay, equal everything. If men want and enjoy sex, then women feel they should too, so they go out and try to be as sexy as men.

Women should not be surprised that they are considered sex objects, because we are inundated with songs of love, such as,

'Keep young and beautiful, if you want to be loved', and love is sex. They have been conditioned by male propaganda to make them believe that giving sexual pleasure to a man is one of their main purposes in life; the measure of their worth is how well they perform. Ninety per cent of the songs a woman hears tell her that she is desirable, that sex is wonderful and that every man wants to make love to her.

If she indicates to a man that she is willing and he doesn't respond, she feels that she is ugly, not worthwhile, a failure. But if the man responds, she feels desirable, worthwhile. She feels she is participating in the glorious act that she was born for, even if it hurts, even if it's not good.

A woman's obsession with beauty is dictated by the need to attract men, and attract they do, but mostly as a sex object. 'The male gaze projects its fantasy on to the female figure which is on display as sexual object.' Men are genetically programmed to be attracted by women with breasts, smooth skin, fine features and a submissive demeanour. The attraction is for sex, and her brain has little to do with his selection.

Women must use their brains to tell themselves that they aren't the same as men; that they were not programmed to enjoy intercourse; that pleasing men sexually, having babies, and raising children is not the road to happiness for most. They probably do have a nurturing instinct, but their brains should tell them to control it if it isn't going to be best for them. They must realize that their purpose in life is to avoid pain and suffering, and that they will find happiness in achieving other goals. Believe in yourself. Do something you love.

Men should also realize that their desire for intercourse is a genetic thing that was once necessary, but not any more. If they think about it, they will come to realize that intercourse is too often a trial and tribulation, and that they would be happier without it. The only hard thing a man should have in his pants is a cellular telephone.

The strongest genetic programme we have is the desire to stay alive. If we know we can overcome that (see the chapter on *Killing is Sometimes OK*), men should realize that it should not be so difficult to overcome the genetic programme to want intercourse and to dominate women. If we are to save the human race we, both men and women, must change our way of life.

If 50,000 years ago *homo sapiens*' females had breasts the size of water melons, if female breast sizes had not changed even into the modern industrial age, and if women had the brains they have today, they would all be promoting genetic engineering and selection to change the female body. They would look at cows and realize that large breasts are not at all best for this generation.

Women were given the vote in North America after World War One and since then have been given a fair amount of equality in politics and the work-place. 'Given' is the correct word. Man is still quite dominant. Until recently, all people in power were men. Fathers were heads of households. Ministers were men. School principals were men. Business executives and bosses were men.

In much of the world a woman is still something for a man to own; a sex object to give him sexual pleasure; someone to wait on him and please him. Women serve, men lead. In some societies a woman even has to provide a dowry to a man who will marry her, and after marriage, if the parents of the bride fail to deliver the dowry, the husband kills the bride. In many societies girl babies are often killed off, because a male baby is wanted.

In other words, man is still an animal. Therefore, in the future, it is quite possible for men to decide that liberated women are no longer to their liking and take away all the female liberties.

You would think that the Nazi philosophy had died after World War Two, but no, the skin-heads of Germany are again trying to bring back the idea of the dominance of the strong over the weak. They should not succeed.

The dominant male baboon will sometimes kill a female baboon, who has allowed a subordinate male to mate with her. This makes sure that only his strong dominant genes will survive. In any case the human female must be aware that it could happen, as indicated by the number of Battered Women Shelters. In fact, today more women are murdered or badly beaten by their husbands or lovers than by strangers. Neanderthal man is extinct, but his attitudes still flourish.

A new kind of evolution is in order, one that gives birth to a frame of mind which acknowledges and accepts the self-evident equal worth of females and males alike. Someday women will be as strong as men, physically and mentally, but until that day comes women must be prepared to live in the strong male world.

One of the main reasons for marriage is to have available reliable and sufficiently frequent sexual encounters. Men's weakness for sex is their 'Achilles heel', and women take advantage of this to get a man to marry them. But if people decide that marriage is a gamble, where the odds for success are small, one will opt for the single state, where the chances for happiness are much greater.

Since the twelfth century, wedlock has been based not on procreation and status, but more and more on love. Today couples who get married only because they love each other are not likely to have a happy marriage. People who fall in love have developed a powerful bond with the object of their sexual attentions. Love is sex plus affection. When you are in love you want to be with the person, and you want to enjoy sex with them, but the passion will not last. You therefore should realize that this is not a good reason to promise to live with them intimately for the rest of your life.

Some feel that without love, life is desolate, the same as an alcoholic feels about ee's drink. In fact, love is a disease like alcoholism or any other addiction and is just as destructive to one's own personality. Love is being obsessed, and it makes one do all manner of things, like getting married. Our senses are flooded every day with the message that love is everything; lonely is a nam without love. Most of the songs that have been written are about the desire for love.

Most novels, movies, radio and TV programmes are about romance and sex and how wonderful it is. And it is wonderful, or in many cases can be, but if you analyze your pleasures, you will find that other things are far more important and pleasurable, such as your hobbies, your sport, your work or your friends.

Love can be a snare and a delusion. So much of it is the joy of having someone think you are wonderful. If you need others to say you are wonderful, you will always be disappointed, unless of course you accept your dog's admiration as conclusive evidence that you are wonderful. You must look in the mirror and say, 'I like me. I am special. No one else is exactly like me.' Sex you can do without.

Humans have survived and prospered, because we are continually being born with the sex drive. It has nothing to do with our happiness. Even if we hadn't enjoyed sex, our genetic drive was there, and as a result our race has survived. However, our sex drive is a force driving us to extinction. Our brains must convince us that this programming must be curbed and controlled. Not having intercourse is not all that bad. Lots of animals have to do without, and they get along. Many of us get along fine without sex.

Anyway, intercourse isn't all that wonderful. Almost all movies, TV, books and songs say it is, but it isn't. Even when you are married, you probably won't have intercourse more than once a week, and later it's more like once a month.

When you are first starting out it can be frightening, traumatic, and for the woman especially, it can hurt or be uncomfortable. You may be scared to death. Some women feel they are married to a man with a heat-seeking missile in his pants.

Later, it can become boring or you can lose your desire altogether, especially for women. So, don't get married for sex. You will seldom be satisfied. Not being married does not guarantee more sex or better sex, but your chances are much better.

If you don't find a partner for sex, it's not the end of the world. Most male mammals don't get much sex. It is only the dominant male who does. It must become quite a chore for him to feel he has to perform so often, and think of all the fights he must endure to maintain his position. If you remember what it was like from puberty through high school and college, if you never got to intercourse, it wasn't bad. You really didn't think about it that much. Nothing happens if you don't. Just put it out of your mind or take a cold shower.

If you can't put it out of your mind you can masturbate. They used to say it was bad for you, but you knew it wasn't. It sure isn't as good as the real thing, but it relieves the urge, the pressure. Some day we will have available a Virtual Reality Sex Suit with sensors and dildoes to give the sensation of intercourse for both male and female. Who knows what lies ahead?

Most human male animals today are genetically programmed to want intercourse with a human female. The desire and urge is very strong and the act is enjoyable, because in the past the genes that were passed on were from males who had these desires. If it weren't for sex, men would prefer to spend most of their time with other men, and women would prefer the company of other women most of the time. If it were not for the pleasure that intercourse gives, we would be better off without it, because of the contraception problems, the danger of the many infectious diseases and the trouble both sexes have in making it pleasurable for the other.

CONSUMPTION IS THE GREAT POLLUTER

In the past, we worked hard and we studied hard in order to get a job that paid enough so we could partake of the good life. We wanted to have a cottage by the water, where the fishing was good, where there was lots of room for water skiing, where the water was clear for scuba-diving, where the drinking water was cool and fresh, where no one locked doors because you felt safe, where everyone knew everyone, and it was not too crowded.

If you had enough money you could have a nice home in the suburbs where you could have a waste-disposal unit, throw-away nappies, clean air, plenty of water for lawns and gardens, throw-away glass or plastic bottles, throw-away cups and dishes and towels, nylon clothing, two cars and outside lighting. This was the good life. Being able to consume is what we have constantly been striving for.

This was to be the measure of our success. We are not likely to give it up even if it takes more and more tax money to get rid of the garbage. When will we learn that we could have it all for fewer dollars, if we only had fewer people?

Today we are supposed to do without nylon clothes in order to use cotton that is grown, not mined. Even if you are rich you can't have many things, because we are generating so much pollution. You shouldn't even leave your lights on or have a second refrigerator, because the electrical power station puts out a great deal of pollution into the air. You can't even continue to work if you are a fishernam, because there aren't enough fish in the sea. You can't play in the sun as much, because ultra-violet rays are stronger now that the ozone layer is being depleted by pollution.

We are running out of fresh water, and the coral in the oceans is being destroyed by pollution. You can't water your lawn or garden enough to keep it alive, and we can't get rid of the garbage from our huge population. If we burn it we cause too much air pollution, and we have run out of space for land-fill sites.

We all keep striving for affluence so we can have more and do more. The more we do, the more energy we use in the form of gasoline for cars and aeroplanes, and natural gas and coal for heating and electrical power.

All of these energy sources spew a great deal of pollution into the air. Our oil and gas are being used up at an alarming rate. We have improved our engines and added catalytic converters, but again this is only pulling us back from the brink.

We really don't know where the brink is with air pollution. We could already be over the hump. The concentration of carbon dioxide in the atmosphere is rising by about 0.5% a year. It is already about 25% higher than pre-industrial levels and may double as soon as the year 2030. A doubling of this gas would increase temperatures around the world to a point where the continuing temperature rise could not be stopped. It would be irreversible and great flooding from melting polar ice would destroy our whole way of life.

Our level of air pollution would not be so bad if we were not cutting down the forest (we have already lost half of the forest which used to cover the earth), and ploughing up much of the grass-land that could convert carbon dioxide into the oxygen humans need to breathe. But we need the forest-cutting, land-ploughing and strip-mining to supply foods and products for our masses. We are taking too many fish from the sea, and we have had to stop cod-fishing off Newfoundland and salmon-fishing off the north west (Washington) coast. Our mines are miles deep and dangerous, and eventually we will run out, or it will become too costly to mine. Our oil is being used up at an alarming rate.

We are on the verge of not having enough fresh water; on the verge of not being able to grow enough food; on the verge of not being able to find enough oil, trees and minerals; on the verge of not being able to get rid of the garbage and waste; on the verge of polluting the air we breathe beyond the possibility of rejuvenation (and this means the extinction of mankind); on the verge of destroying the ozone layer; on the verge of making so many animal and insect species extinct, because we are forever expanding humans into their habitat. Why must we be on the verge?

We cannot rely on science to keep coming up with stop-gap measures to pull us back from the brink. Even nuclear power hasn't accomplished its hoped-for goal, because of cost and the problem of waste disposal.

However, if our population were much smaller, say two-thirds smaller, then the required amount of forest-cutting, land-ploughing and strip-mining would not be a problem for the environment. We don't need so many people. Each one of us would be happier and better off if we had fewer people. Why would people want to stay on the brink of disaster?

As long as we keep increasing our population with its inherent consumption and garbage, the greater problem we will have finding land-fill sites. Even if our population stayed as it is, we would have an unsolvable problem. We try to conserve and recycle, but it is a drop in the ocean. Most of it still ends up in the garbage.

If our consumption of oil, natural gas, coal, metals, chemicals and other non-renewable resources is doubling every 20 years, then by the year 1990 we might have used up half of what was there originally. And if we are still using up double the amount of the year before, we will have used it all up by the year 2010 (see example below).

If in 1850 we had a volume of 254 (just a fictitious figure):

Year	Volume used every 20 years	Total volume used
1870	1	1
1890	2	3
1910	4	7
1930	8	15
1950	16	31
1970	32	63
1990	64	127 = half used up
2010	128	255 = all used up

When you have used up half your resources it takes only one more time interval to use it all up. Of course we don't know how much is down there, and after a while the mines will get so deep that they won't be economical. In any case the concept is scary, and we shouldn't wait until we have long line-ups and high prices for gasoline before the drastic situation gets our attention and holds it.

For many thousands of years the human population has been small enough that nature was able to handle the waste. Gradually our population grew to the point where our waste could not be handled by nature. Factories and mills spew out toxic waste into the rivers and lakes in such quantities that marine life is killed off and the water can't be made pure enough to drink. The scale of resource consumption is increasing environmental costs faster than it increases production benefits.

We have made sewage treatment plants, but never enough to compensate for the ever-growing population. Treatment plants are expensive. People must work many hours to make enough money to pay enough taxes to pay for the treatment plants. Our taxes are already a high percentage of our income. They might have to go higher still to keep the air pure and endangered species alive. If the ecological costs rise faster than benefits, we are getting poorer rather than richer. If we didn't have to spend the money on treatment plants, it could be used for pleasurable pursuits.

Before humans were on the scene there wasn't any population problem. Each animal had as much body waste as humans have today, but they were few in number. If their numbers did grow too large, nature took over to restore a better balance. The fish and mammals in the seas and lakes produce body waste, but their numbers have never exceeded what the waters could easily handle.

All living things are genetically programmed to reproduce their kind. If they weren't, they would die out. Only a few animals that are hatched or born survive to propagate. The elephant, lion and shark have a relatively low rate of reproduction but have an adequate food supply and few enemies. The cod-fish egg has only about 1 in 14 million chances of survival, but one pair of cod produce a sufficient number of fertilized eggs each time for the species to survive (as long as nam does not harvest too many).

No organism is capable of ravaging the very ecosystem in which it evolved without destroying itself. When population overcrowding occurs, the whole social structure of the animal is destroyed by disease – killing off the young – and fighting, until the population is drastically cut back or destroyed.

When the crown-of-thorn population increases dramatically in an area, the starfish take over, and soon the crown-of-thorn population is decimated.

Naturalists have known for some time that animals will reproduce in such numbers that, if all survived to reproduce again, and those reproduced again and increased exponentially, they would soon over-run the earth. However, this does not happen because they run out of food, or their habitat is changed so that their death rate is accelerated, and sometimes they die out. Nature, red in tooth and claw, forces a balance.

The human birth-rate of one every year is quite low, but the species survived because we were able to take care of our young. The women were pregnant most of the time and bore enough children to take care of larger farms and livestock and to replace those who died. The population did not grow very fast until the industrial revolution began around 1770, when food supply and health improved, and then it started to grow and grow and grow.

Unfortunately, the balancing forces do not apply as strongly to humans. Our brains have allowed us to devise ways to circumvent these forces in order to support a massive population, partly by defeating many sicknesses and prolonging life. Humans have prospered, thus far, and our numbers have grown, but we have gone too far. The growing human population today will soon destroy our air, water and other life support systems and we will die out unless we reduce our population. We should realize that we are destroying the other animals, and this should be seen to be as bad as Hitler's wanting to destroy the Jews, Cortez destroying the Aztecs, or whites destroying African blacks by slavery.

We should not want to be a member of a society which believes might is right. Just because we could destroy most of the animals, it doesn't mean we should. We need the animals. The North American Indian respected animals and trees, and so should we. Humans are only a part of nature where all things are inter-dependent. We are not here to dominate the world and all the animals as suggested in the bible. We have no more right to be here than other animals.

Our population has grown to huge proportions, and we have killed off many animals including the buffalo, birds, most of the wild animals of Africa, and many of the North American animals as well as the Indians. Even today it is estimated that human activity causes the extinction of at least 20,000 species of plants and animals every year. We humans originally killed animals for food, but we don't need to do that now. No other animal goes out to kill and destroy another species. Destroying the animals' habitat and limiting their space is something that only nam does.

Many people have an overwhelming desire to see open space changed into a land which supports new communities filled with homes and children. Many of these are religious people who feel we should accommodate as many souls as possible, because humans with souls are God's chosen to be immortal. Each human life is precious, and we must preserve as many as possible. Well, if we do try to keep all these souls going, the resulting pollution would cause the extinction of the human race. If there is no such thing as a soul, this whole idea would be a doubly destructive preoccupation.

If population growth is a problem of the under-developed countries (which now constitute four-fifths of the world's population), consumption is the curse of the remaining one-fifth. Under-developed means they don't have subways, six lane highways, millions of cars, tall sky-scrapers, and stores full of items no-one really needs.

Europe, North America and Japan consume two-thirds of the world's energy, and account for four-fifths of the world's waste, and the consumption rate of the rich countries is 20 times that of the developing world. One Canadian has about the same environmental impact through resource exploitation and pollution as 50 people in India.

Just think what would happen if the under-developed masses became developed. The results would be catastrophic. Water and air pollution all over the world would start to cause deaths in the millions of all living things. There is a good chance that even after billions die off the air and water would have been so damaged that they would not recover.

If these people simply had doctors, health-care, good food-growing land, water and a few manufacturing plants, their people would probably have a happier life-style than the so-called affluent society. It would be like our living out in the country close to nature. Oh, what a dream.

If we want to stop the depletion of our energy resources, the extinction of animal species, the pollution of the ozone layer, air, oceans, lakes, rivers and land, there is only one answer: population reduction. For humans to survive into the distant future, we must bring our numbers down to be in a sustained harmony with the ecology.

OVER-POPULATION WILL DESTROY

Because of massive immigration and an ever-increasing birth-rate, our population is growing out of control. People have to go somewhere, but a city should realize that the people already there are not going to be happier if more people are added. It just cuts down on the convenience of living. No-one is happier for having 4.2 million people in Metropolitan Toronto. If you are standing in the smog of the city, or if you are stuck in traffic for hours, you begin to ask yourself: 'If this is development, who needs it?' We can't keep growing forever.

Politicians measure their success by the industrial growth they have achieved in their area. This growth is supposed to be good. It creates jobs for the new influx of people, but we end up with more of the same: packed housing and streets, tall buildings and multilane highways.

The more people we have, the more football and hockey clubs we need to accommodate the large number of spectators. We used to have just the right number of clubs. We knew the stars and names of all the players in every club. Now there are so many, one is likely to get discouraged and give up.

Toronto was founded because its good farming soil would attract settlers, little knowing the region would become all settlers and no farms. When the Municipality of Metropolitan Toronto was formed in 1953, there were still many farms within its borders, enough to contain any growth for the foreseeable future. Well, foreseeable has been here for some time.

It took only 15 years for Toronto to grow from 2 million to 3 million, a 50% increase even when the number of babies per couple was maybe 2.5. Some of the growth, no doubt, was due to immigration. There are 4.2 million of us living in the region now, and we are still growing. We are not as New York City with its 17 million inhabitants but we are already three times too big. When we look at today's world, we can see only an uncertain future for our children. Therefore, please work for the survival of our race by making a reduction in population your goal.

If our world had only 2 billion people, and everyone had about the same standard of living, we could have a high standard of living without causing damage to our air and water. A population larger than that is bound to produce too much pollution.

Back when people were old at 40 and the death rate was high, they were having many children per couple, but the population did not increase rapidly. Today, we are not dying until 70 or 80 years old, and our population is growing at an alarming rate, even when we are having fewer children per couple. There are more people living today than have been born since the Egyptian pharaohs.

World population

Year	Billion		
1850	1		
1930	2	(doubled in 80 years)	(12 million increase per year)
1974	4	(doubled in 44 years)	(45 million increase per year)
1993	5.6		(84 million increase per year)

World population is now increasing at the rate of 100 million per year. Even if all couples started today to have no more than two children, the population would continue to increase until about the year 2050, because our population has far more young people than old people. It's like trying to run up the down-escalator. At present growth-rate, our population will be 10 billion by the year 2035 – double our present population – and 14 billion by the year 2100. You can't imagine the devastation this will cause.

The Canadian province of Quebec should be severely criticized for its attempt to use economic incentives to encourage the birth rate of its French-speaking population. This is the height of irresponsibility. The survival of the Francophone culture would be better served if they limited immigration to people speaking the French language.

Most of the population growth is in the so-called under-developed countries, such as India and many countries in Africa, where women bear over six children on average. China, for instance, tripled its population in one lifetime. In 1900 it had 1 billion. In 1990 it had 3 billion. At least it is now trying to reduce population by attempting to limit each couple to only one child.

Contraception for the under-developed world is a good idea. It will give some protection from AIDS, but it probably won't stop the population growth, because the females still have only one purpose in life and that is to be mothers. Until a woman's purpose in life is changed, there is little hope of population reduction.

If we in North America were able to reduce our population, and the rest of the world kept growing in numbers, we would not be able to save ourselves. We simply could not survive with polluted oceans and polluted air all around us. We can only hope that the others will see the danger in time. Life continuing on earth is not a sure thing.

It would take only a few large atomic bombs exploding anywhere on earth to destroy the atmosphere. A large meteorite hitting the earth would do the same thing. If AIDS were more contagious, we might all be dying. If antibiotics became ineffective against some germ mutations, it could spell the end of human life. But let us not worry about things we have no control over. Let's try to do our best to make life better for future generations, in case there is a future.

As soon as we start to reduce our population, there will be a great problem with the economy. Can you imagine what will happen to the value of housing or rental space when the population is shrinking? The opposite of a baby boom would mean fewer products needed, less manufacturing, fewer stores, fewer jobs etc. Some of this sort of thing is happening today because of the computer, the information highway, etc.

We adapt to changes usually because the changes do not occur overnight. Our population reduction will almost certainly be a slow process, and where some items become less in demand, other new items will take their place. If sofraternities become ever more popular, the need for family housing will decrease.

A gradual change is recommended, but not too slow. We have a long way to go even to get the increasing population to stabilize. After that we can proceed with a gradual reduction. Let's concentrate on North America, and that means controlling birth rate and immigration, the two main factors in population stability, assuming the death rate stays relatively the same.

Immigration should be immediately reduced to zero. Maybe we could accept immigrant relatives for a short time, but no longer should we be a permanent haven for refugees, even the ones who are liable to be killed in their own country. There is no shortage of people trying to flee their strife-torn or poverty-stricken countries, but we do not owe the entire world unlimited access to our shores. Babies born in Canada should only get Canadian citizenship if the mother is Canadian. Our raft is already over-loaded. Any more and we all sink.

We should not have immigration for the purpose of cheap labour to do jobs our people do not want to do. If our people do not wish to do certain jobs because the pay is low, increase the wage. If this increases the cost of the product too much, don't make it. If people can't afford the higher price, they will do without or use something else.

Immigration should not be used to bring money into the country. Our population control is more important. We must control our population if we are to provide health-care for all, housing and financial aid to the poor. The answer to our problem is doing the logical thing.

North America's immigration policy has made us a 'melting pot' but we will become a 'melt-down' if we don't eliminate immigration and reduce births. If we don't do it by ourselves, it will be done for us by nature, and it will be done brutally and without pity.

We need more doctors to advertise: 'Don't add to human over-population. For low cost vasectomy and hysterectomy, call +++ ++++.'

BABY MAKERS

The only way to reduce population is for women to stop having so many babies. The human female is programmed to want to have children, to nurture and bring up a family. Females for thousands of years have felt that they were not fulfilled, and were not fulfilling their destiny, unless they had children. Women still feel that their breasts are for suckling babies, and that if they carry around breasts all the time they should have some babies. They are reminded that they are the baby suppliers when they menstruate each month. Their wide hips are good for bending over to gather food, gardening, having babies and carrying young children. Therefore, they feel that their prime role is to have babies.

Females were programmed to be soft, delicate and submissive, and these features got the males to give them as many babies as required for the survival of the human race. But 'survival of the fittest' does not mean 'survival of the happiest'. It is only in the last hundred years that some female brains have begun to realize that many women will not find real happiness in having babies. For many, it is a responsibility that does not lead to the best life. Being submissive and cared for by a male is not what they want, and they find that they can be forceful and in charge and they can compete in the male world.

Women may not overcome their programming unless other factors come into prominence, such as a great desire to reduce the population by having fewer babies. Just because women don't have brawn doesn't mean they don't have brains that can overcome this programming. Roberta Bondar (an astronaut) said, 'The children aspect will not be part of my biological contribution to the world.'

It certainly does not make any of us happier to have crowds of people around us on the highway, in the air, destroying wild animal habitat, polluting land, sea and air. We should aim to reduce our population to one-third of the 6 billion we have today. We must stop having so many babies, or mankind is doomed to extinction.

A woman's desire to have babies is one of the greatest dangers to human survival. If our populations continue to grow, we will drown in our own pollution. The greenhouse effect will become non-reversible; the ozone layer could be destroyed and us with it; polluted water will kill us; or general waste will overwhelm us.

Why continue to live on the edge of disaster? For their own good and the good of the human experience, women must change their desire to be nurturing mothers.

Women should look on being pregnant as similar to being sick with scarlet fever. If a male sperm enters your body it can result in a disease called sperm fever. It produces swelling, increase in weight, nausea, headache, heartburn, food craving, and is exhausting. The immediate treatment for sperm fever is a surgical procedure called an abortion. It involves the removal of a foetus.

A surgical procedure done maybe nine months after getting sperm fever, is called a caesarean section. It involves the removal of an infant who has developed from the foetus. The alternative to a surgical treatment is to let the disease run its course, which takes about nine months.

To avoid getting sperm fever, a doctor's recommendation is the same as to avoid getting many other contagious diseases; stay away from people, specifically men; don't let an unsheathed penis get into your vagina; take the prescribed pills or get an inoculation against the disease; or have a hysterectomy.

Both men and women are conditioned (brainwashed) by our society to feel that having and raising children is the most rewarding, wonderful and fulfilling thing in life. Most of all they assume that to be a good, responsible, worthwhile, patriotic person, you must have a home with spouse and children. A man doesn't feel truly a grown-up man unless he has children, and a woman feels like an old maid if she doesn't have children. In some societies the programming is so strong that a woman who dies before marrying is buried in a bridal gown with a doll by her side, representing the child she will never have, all in order that she won't go to heaven with an unfulfilled soul.

Both sexes feel that they must pass on their genes for some kind of immortality. It's a matter of pride, a measure of success. They think of children as pets to be cuddled and played with. They are an expensive hobby, but primarily they have something to be dominant over, to control, and they call it love. Unfortunately, the sins of the parents fall on the children.

Love, sex, weather and children are the four most talked about subjects other than money, but it is the children who are said to be the most important part of a mother or father's life. Few human emotions can equal the joy a parent feels when a son or daughter grows up to be an accomplished, warm and loving person. A parent will say, 'my children are the most precious; the most rewarding; the light of my life; deserving of all my love and attention; the most joy to come home to; the only real thing in my life.' But it is also true that all parents feel they must say these things so that other people will think well of them.

It is hoped that before too long, young women who have been working in our competitive world, and have seen the advantage of being independent, will start to consider the negative aspects of being a mother. Freed from the tyranny of the womb, women may cast off submissive roles that deny them political and economic powers. The women's movement should adopt the word 'unified' as their clarion call. 'All for one, and one for all.'

It is time for men to realize that things have changed, and we must use our superior brains to overcome our programming. Men should have no direct responsibility except to argue and vote for what they feel to be best, unless, of course, they decide to withhold sperm, which would not be a bad idea.

The joys of motherhood have always been stressed, and the joy is real in many cases, but along with the joy is an awful lot of tedium, pain and suffering, both mental and physical. To start with you have taken the biggest gamble of your life. A spouse was the first gamble, but the biggest is what kind of a child you get. You have to take what comes. Taking on responsibility for another means you can't be free to reach for your own goals. If your aim is happiness, don't take responsibility. Don't get married.

A pregnant woman is pregnant for nine months, during which time great changes are taking place. She gets bigger and heavier, and is finally just waddling around with sore feet. Her joints loosen; her hair falls out; her contact lenses don't fit; her bones start to get brittle. She has nausea, vomiting, back pain and headaches. She should not smoke or drink and can't take many medications, and she has to live with it 24 hours a day.

Deciding when to go to the hospital, and getting there in time, is a problem. Each contraction is like a severe muscle cramp, and she knows she will have another in a few minutes. In many cases she has to have a caesarean section which means a cutting open and sewing up and all the hazards of an operation. And then the biggest hazard of all is the baby's health.

You may not know the percentages, but the odds are far too great that you could have twins, Siamese twins, a Down's Syndrome child, or a child who is disabled in another way who will require constant care and whose life will always be a struggle and heartache for both parents and child.

And that is just the beginning of the pain and suffering, the long hours of hard labour, the disappointments. Some changes in women's bodies are permanent, including stretch marks, drooping breasts and bigger hips. If men had to have babies, our race would quickly disappear. Do women have any doubts about that?

How will the reduction in population come about, if it does? It could happen that a majority of men and women in a country could become convinced that a reduction in population was essential. With a majority, they could promote their aim, possibly by the use of government money (tax money) to influence others. Governments can help reduce our population by having no tax incentives for having unauthorized children; no restrictions on abortion; no baby bonuses. If they cannot afford to take care of their children, the children would be placed in a sofraternity. Let's show others that it can be done. It has to be done.

Somewhere along the line, sufficient stress should be placed on women to have fewer or no children. A woman's right to have children should not be regulated, but ways to influence her would probably be tried. Some women will think that having and raising children does not have a high enough percentage of good, so if society wants some children, society should make it financially worthwhile.

Some day, if women have used their brains to overcome the maternal instinct, and feel they can have a more enjoyable existence without child-bearing, they will leave the child-bearing to women who choose to do it as their profession. Women bearing children with acceptable genes would be paid a good salary. Acceptable genes would be any female eggs and male sperm that were assumed to be free of defective genes that could cause medical problems for a child. It is assumed that the rules would not restrict race or any group in any way. Rather it would promote the use of genes to produce good characteristics.

The idea of females pair-bonding for life with a male is something that our species developed socially just by chance. If things and circumstances had been different, human females might have been programmed to be like many other animals.

The most radical blueprint could have been bees, where the queen is the only one in the colony to produce offspring, and she can choose to make males or females. She makes mostly only females, but chemically treats each one so that none can reproduce, and they all become workers. So, if human females are smart they will not continue on with the genetic and social programming that is no longer best for the individual's happiness, but will try to change things for the better. Presumably this would be to have a specialized group being the baby-makers and a professional group the child-rearers.

A zipper should be developed for the women baby-makers, and at the end of the first caesarean birth the zipper would be stitched in. For subsequent births, unzip the zipper and out comes the baby. Women would then no longer need wide hips. Maybe we could inseminate cows with human fertilized eggs and let them bear our children.

Women should take charge of the population problem. If all women decided not to have any more children, the human race would die out in approximately 125 years. This would be a bit extreme, and would not happen, but it shows that women, and only women, have the future of the human race in their hands. This would leave many horny old men, but it would work. Women should decide what population numbers are best, and make it happen.

Right now if all women had two babies each, our population would continue to grow and then level off. Even if we had only one birth per woman on average, it would take a long time to reduce our population to 2 billion. The result would be the same if half the women had two babies and the other half had none.

We will finally be making progress when more and more women see the big advantage in not having babies. Maybe only one out of five will have five babies or less, or one out of ten will have ten babies or less. Maybe by genetic manipulation, instead of having an equal number of males and females, fewer females will be born. This would definitely solve the problem.

The women who wish to not have any, or any more, children, have a problem. Abstinence, of course, is best. This does not preclude sex and orgasm. It merely means no intercourse, unless the male has a vasectomy. Pills, IUDs, condoms and diaphragms are also available, but the woman must make a definite decision. If she fails, there is always abortion, but this is a poor alternative. There are many groups, like the Catholic Church, who are against all methods except abstinence, so some women may run into roadblocks.

If too much oestrogen from birth-control pills (passing through the body) gets into drinking water, or if we just lace drinking water with pills, we may have no trouble reducing population.

RAISING CHILDREN

Many animals, such as the turtle, never see their young. Some animals eat their young, the male lion for instance. The female lion, when she makes a kill, allows other lions to feed in order of their hierarchy in the pride. Her young are the last to feed and sometimes they starve. The female lion, however, is most ferocious in protecting her young from the male lions and other predators. Many species have survived with some peculiar traits. The human animal might not have survived if the male had not been programmed to feed and protect the mother and children while the children were growing up.

Certainly, taking care of your offspring can have some enjoyable times, but for many parents it's a frustrating grind. You fear you are not doing a good job when you can't control your offspring and are even afraid of them. Sometimes kids just laugh in your face when you try to discipline them.

It's not enjoyable changing nappies and getting urinated on; having the baby feed on sore nipples; taking half an hour to try to feed a monster who keeps spitting out every spoonful; watching the food bowl being shoved off the high-chair tray.

It's frustrating throwing a ball to a kid who can't catch, not knowing what to do when a one-year-old cries as soon as you try to leave the room at night after many good-night stories, hugs and kisses, or what to do when a child doesn't obey or do ee's chores, or doesn't show any love, affection or appreciation.

It's tough deciding how much allowance to give and what it can be used for. How many things and pleasures should you give up in order that the child can have clothes, medical care, education, etc. What sports, activities and jobs must you give up because some danger exists, and you don't want your child to grow up without a father or mother.

There is not much pleasure watching the children grow up in the rear-view mirror; having to cheer, coach, and chaperone for all the activities – swimming, choir, dancing, Brownies, piano, baseball, hockey, etc; having to get them all dressed and not forget something; shelling out the money for all this when it leaves so little for yourself; not having time for your own activities; having to help with homework; listening to someone learning the trumpet; having to keep your good china or anything breakable out of sight; not being able to go out without a sitter; getting up in the middle of the night for feeding, bed wetting and sickness.

One of the major problems for the small nuclear family is how to control the children. How late can they stay out and what penalty should be applied if they're late? When the youngster or teenager does something wrong, or doesn't do as ee is told, what should parents do? What is suitable punishment, and what would bring the desired results? To spank or not to spank, that is the question.

In most families, whatever they try doesn't seem to work, and in many cases they go to extremes rather than admit they can't control their kids. In a sofraternity setting this should be less of a problem. The rules would be the same for all, and the children would not be saying, 'Jimmy's mother doesn't make him do that.'

How often have you seen mothers slapping, shouting at, and dragging their kids in the supermarkets and malls, calling them 'dummies', 'brats' or worse? How often have teachers seen many battered and disturbed children in their classroom? One gets the impression that the ability to be a good parent does not come with mother's milk.

A young parent today is less well-informed and more ill-at-ease about problems concerning childhood than the parent of any prior generation. The average middle-class mother is a product of a small family and has had little, if any, contact with babies and young children.

Letting fathers and mothers have dictatorial powers over children is dangerous. Some parents have sex with their children. Some children are beaten and disfigured, starved, made to work very hard, brainwashed to believe all sorts of things, refused medical aid, and kept in religious cults. Those who have power and authority over the vulnerable will abuse it in grotesque and ruthless ways, just because they can, and this is the root cause of sexual abuse.

Right-to-life advocates should be out picketing for a child's right to life, liberty, and the pursuit of happiness, and not life under a dictatorial parent. One of life's strangest ironies is that you need a licence to drive a car, and you have to convince authorities of your qualifications to adopt a child, but any women can have a baby. In other words, children should be brought up by professional parents, who have been trained for the job.

We are finding today that child physical and sexual abuse is far more prevalent than expected. This is very evident when you count the number of drop-in centres there are for incest victims, hostels for pregnant teenagers, and shelters for run-away kids. The number of teenagers who run away each year in the US is 1.3 million (1990). A child is so vulnerable when <u>ee</u> is dominated by a parent. The child is afraid and feels <u>ee</u> is responsible for not pleasing enough. The need to please is so strong the child will let a parent do anything, thinking the parent is all-powerful and wise.

A child brought up in a home where it sees stress handled by anger, will likely grow up to do the same. Young people see their parents smoking and, like the early explorers who saw Indians smoking, they want to try it. When they do, they usually don't enjoy it at first, but they think they are not grown-up unless they do, so they keep going until they are hooked. However, in a sofraternity situation this should not occur.

Some will say that at home a child can get nurturing, and in an institution <u>ee's</u> just a number, but the trouble is that so many parents won't or can't give the necessary nurturing, especially a single parent. A considerable number of parents are not taking care of their children, and many kids are out on the street after midnight. More children are killed at home by parents than out on the street, so children should be brought up in sofraternities. In a sofraternity the care-person would be trained and supervised to give the proper care children so desperately need.

The future is bleak if we don't take care of our kids. In the past many have suggested getting the children into expanded day-care facilities as early as 2 years old. This would help, but it is not a long-term solution. All children, if possible, should be in a sofraternity home where they can get a good and loving upbringing.

The nuclear family was always primarily for the production and rearing of children. If our society decides that we can't continue to have children in anywhere near the old numbers, then the need for the nuclear family is greatly reduced. Since one or two children, brought up by one stay-at-home mother, is not good and no longer workable, we need to find a way to raise children properly.

Today young children are kept in day-care centres. Children are taught in schools for six or more hours a day, plus extra-curricular activities. In college, children are mostly away from home except during holidays. In other words, our children are brought up outside the home to a large extent. What we need is an extended family group better than a boarding school, something comprehensive and caring.

The organization should be specifically designed to be responsible for the children 24 hours a day, from birth through all the necessary schooling. Professionally trained and dedicated people should be ready and anxious to give lots of TLC (Tender Loving Care) and create a sincere bonding with the children.

Not long ago children were underfoot at home only until they could start doing chores or when they could be out doing a day's work in the field, in the mine or mill. They were maybe only 7 years old, and schooling was minimal.

Today our society is not like other mammals, where the young are with the mother for only a year or less before they are on their own, and may never see their mother again. Our society has become so complicated that the child has to be in school until ee is 18 or older, a quarter of the person's life span. During this long period the child is going through many stages which a mother or father is not equipped to handle.

Genetically we, as parents, were programmed to take care of the children, to feed, house and clothe them. This was necessary for survival. As our numbers grew and our society grew, the child-care years stretched out far beyond the original genetic intent. Back then, they didn't have a society that allowed us to make a better arrangement, but today we do.

Our present day school system tries very hard to give each child equal opportunity, but it is an impossibility because of the child's environment outside of school. Think of the differences: being brought up rich or poor (children from well-off families are most likely to be near the top of their class); white or dark (it's still a white man's world); in a tender, caring, helpful family compared with a hateful, cruel, domineering or ignorant atmosphere. In a sofraternity the chances of equal opportunity are so much greater.

If we don't make changes, both women and children will be in trouble. A single parent working or a couple both working, with one or more children to worry about, is bound to be seen as a poor arrangement for both parents and children. Working parents haven't got the time, skills, and patience, and one child without a lot of brothers and sisters is not good.

The child should at all times be under the care and supervision of the professionals who would live in, work, and be paid by the sofraternity and to some extent by the government, just as school teachers are now. This would continue until the child finishes ee's schooling. The professionals would be like day-care, and probably work in 8-hour shifts. These would be people who want to be involved with children, just like 'big brothers' do today.

Schooling may extend into kindergarten and some lower grades, depending on the number of children in the sofraternity. The children would probably go outside for the higher grades, high school, and university.

A mother should not have to live in the sofraternity with the child, but she probably would want to maintain an interest and an association with the child. In the early years of this transition, there will still be parents who want to bring up their children in their own home. But if the sofraternity idea grew to a majority, as it must if we are to get a reduction in our population, the government would probably discourage the old arrangement by providing funding for only sofraternity type environments.

We should have genetic testing available for all births in order to check for a variety of diseases and problems. Records would be kept showing father and mother for future gene pool references, plus finger prints for identification. In future, you will not be tracing your lineage by your name so much as by your genetic history.

It could become law that only genetically approved babies would be funded, and women would only be paid to have babies if they had followed all the rules, such as no smoking and no alcohol. It would be expected that professionals of the sofraternity would be 'family' to these children for always. If there were changes, it would not be as often as today's broken homes and multiple marriages. Plus, each child would have more than one or two parents.

The rearing and education of children is the most important factor in producing a happy society. Certainly the blame for the lack of a happy society today, to a large extent, can be placed on the way our parents raised us, and to some extent our teachers. Of course many were quite good, but too many were not. There was too little attention, much too much abuse, both physical, mental and sexual, and too much poor example. Children need good role models so they will strive for the best.

A larger number of adults should be taking care of infants than of older children. By the end of the first three years, a child's whole personality is said already to be established. But even in the crib the child needs stimulation by touching, cuddling, talking, sounds and eye-catching movement. Later, the emphasis would be on praise and encouragement for the activities they do well.

Children should be involved in activities so they will develop a certain degree of confidence and proficiency. Parents have not done well in teaching subjects like the 'Golden Rule', even with the best of intentions. Some tried to rely on Sunday School, scouting and day-care.

In a sofraternity, the children could not only be told what is best, what is expected of them and why, but the professionals could arrange to have the children put into situations where they have an opportunity to practice what they have been taught. They must have practice in doing the right thing, so it will become their normal response.

Reading and arithmetic are necessary, as well as other basic skills, but since children are taught to print in the earliest grades, why are they ever taught to write long-hand 'cursive writing'? All our typing, books, magazines, computer print-outs and papers are in print. Printing can be written just as fast as writing and is easier to read, so why teach long-hand writing?

Educators should emphasize and teach 'critical thinking' and not try to get students to learn too many of the details of each subject. So much information has been discovered, especially in the last 100 years, that the load on students has become overwhelming. Don't make children re-invent the wheel. The basics of all subjects should be taught but many of the details should only be mentioned. Students should learn just enough to understand a subject so that they know what is available and how to look up and get detailed answers from books or the computer databank.

Emphasis should be placed on finding out what various occupations are all about. They should visit job-sites to learn what really goes on. They should be exposed to enough of each subject so they can decide if they would like to specialize in one specific area of the subject.

People have such a variety of abilities. Some are not very good at remembering names, spelling, mechanical things, arithmetic etc. Nevertheless, these same people might be good at analyzing and logical thinking, musical instrument playing, or musical composition, story-telling, writing, selling or research. Some people have photographic memories and can read a poem of several pages, and after the third reading, have it memorized, yet some of those use poor grammar in speaking or writing.

Some people can improve their memory by association. On a long trip in the car, some of you have played 'Johnnie has in his pocket' where the first person starts with 'Johnnie has an apple in his pocket.' The second person says, 'Johnnie has an apple and a toothpick in his pocket.' Each person adds an object each time their turn arrives. The best way to remember all the objects in proper sequence is by association, by making a picture in your mind as each item is added. You picture the toothpick stuck in the apple. One person said they went through a total of 80 items on one trip.

To remember names of people, make an association. For instance, for Mrs Hummic, make the association with 'stomach', but of course be careful not to remember 'belly' and call her Mrs Kelly by mistake!

For most people, repetition is the best aid to memory. It is like walking in a forest. If a short time later you walk that way again, you can see where the grass was pushed down by your feet and can find your way to your destination. If you do not come back soon enough, the signs are not there to follow any more. If you walk that way often and wear a good path, you can come back years later and still find the path. The brain works the same way. You should make a point of searching out that memory often enough that you wear a good path to that memory, so even years later you will still be able to recall that memory.

A father and his 10-year-old daughter were on a tour of Castle Loma in Toronto, when the daughter said she wished she could remember the name of the tour guide (Cynthia Williams) and also the name of the man who built the castle (Sir Henry Pellet). The father, a few minutes later, asked her to remember the names, and she did. During the tour he asked her to remember a number of times. On the way home, he asked her, and then a day later, then a week later, a month later, a year later, and today she is still able to remember.

Young girls often feel cheated because they don't have a penis that sticks out. They probably have not seen many. Some are so small you can't see them, some as thin as your finger and some a foot long. Have you ever heard a man, who has just sat down on the toilet, exclaim: 'God! That water's cold'?

Girls should be happy they have no genitals hanging down between their legs as they can be very painful when hit. They should also be told that before too long they will have something else that sticks out and is far more noticeable and attractive than a boy's penis. They do have an equivalent to a penis and testicles, only it's inside-out and up inside. This can be demonstrated by having a soft rubber tube that looks like a penis and putting a finger in and pulling it inside-out. Now it looks like a vagina. The head of the penis, when inside-out, is somewhat like the female cervix at the end of the vagina.

Furthermore, the female has two ovaries, one on each side, that produce the eggs, somewhat like the two male testes that produce sperm. An egg comes down the fallopian tube once a month into the woman's uterus. The sperm come down the male penis when he has an ejaculation. If the sperm get into a woman's vagina and work their way up into her uterus and connect with the egg, the egg is fertilized and a baby starts to grow.

Sex education should be real and as thorough as the age would indicate. All forms of sexual activity should be shown and discussed, including homosexuality and all methods of contraception, especially abstinence. American President, Bill Clinton, says masturbation and sexual behaviour should not be taught in schools. Apparently, at the moment, it would be approved only if it is associated with love, respect, affection, reproduction and marriage. But young people should be told that the desire for intercourse is a genetic programme in all animals. At a certain age the desire becomes very strong, and they should be prepared to cope with it.

Approval of sexual pleasure need not lead to licentiousness (lack of restraint), because they would be told of the dangers of AIDS and other forms of sexually transmitted diseases. Even in China, where intercourse has always been regarded as a means to produce more workers, they are now teaching that sex should be a source of pleasure.

When a girl tells a boy that he is nice or has done something to please her, the boy is likely to feel funny and blush. Blushing is a reaction built into the body by genes. The boy can't help it. It just happens. Blood vessels in the skin open up and more blood rushes to his face causing the redness.

The same kind of thing happens to a boy's penis when he sees a pretty girl that he thinks likes him. Automatically, sometimes, his penis gets enlarged, and longer, and stiff, and he gets an ache in his gut. He knows that the girl could make him feel so much better if she would rub his penis inside her vagina. He can't help it. His genes have made him react that way, and he is simply responding to what is expected of him.

The girl would have a similar, but maybe less powerful, reaction if the boy appeals to her. Blood rushes to her vulva around her vaginal opening, and she gets an ache in her gut that makes her want to have her area rubbed by the boy.

Sexual tension (a good word for it) for a man is like a spring that is tightly wound. It hurts when the spring is released, and it takes just a little time to unwind with great feeling. When unwound the man becomes relaxed and falls into a debilitated and sleepy state. An erection is, in one way, something like a muscle cramp. When you get it and don't want it, it takes a little doing to make it relax.

In the ancient animal world, for instance, a genetic change occurred to produce some green monkeys, and these green monkeys prospered and grew in numbers, and if gradually a genetic change took place to make the males less anxious to have intercourse, then in that case the number of babies would get fewer and fewer and that race would die out. Maybe that is why we don't see any green monkeys or even green humans. In other words we wouldn't be here as a human race of whatever colour if we did not still have this genetic programme that makes us want to have intercourse.

Sex education should be a normal part of growing up. Children should be taught about enjoying the pleasurable capacities of the body. This is formalized in central Polynesia where young boys are instructed in the appropriate erotic art by older women. Pleasure is an evolutionary entitlement, and therefore people should expect to enjoy sexual pleasure as a right.

It should not be how it was before Masters and Johnson started the trend to write about sex. Before that, the penis, and the female genitals and intercourse were taboo subjects. Movies showed separate beds for married couples and nothing beyond the kiss was shown. They got married and lived happily ever after. Nudity was forbidden, and at the end of the film love conquered all.

However, AIDS has changed all that. Safe sex has now become the byword, and to teach young people about the use of the condom required that we talk about the penis. This is good, but is far short of what sex education should be. Sex education should include what to do, rather than only what not to do. Sex is something that should be understood and appreciated. Girls should be told about the blood that will come from their vaginas, and boys should be told that they probably will have dreams causing semen to come out of the penis when they are asleep.

Animals don't have any problem seeing and hearing what sex is all about. Before they have any urges, they see and learn about what goes on. Humans are animals, and there is no good reason why they should continually hide their bodies with clothing. Most African and Polynesian tribes did not. Hiding and keeping the subject secret and behind closed doors only promotes the idea that this is the forbidden fruit, something so wonderful and dangerous that only those chosen by God to be married are worthy and ready to take on this wonderful responsibility.

It sure hasn't worked, and certainly it hasn't been good. It has caused such awful hang-ups and frustrations. Two virgins embarking on a sexual relationship have about as much chance of having a catastrophe as two unlicensed kids driving down the highway.

Since the penis has already been mentioned, why not also proclaim that male babies should not be circumcised at birth unless there is some medical reason for it. No one should be subjected to a hurtful procedure without just cause. All the foreskin needs is to be rinsed with water twice a week to keep it clean. It is useful to push back and forth over the tip during masturbation to achieve orgasm, and also to catch the semen.

Sex, as pure entertainment, as an art form, and a means of gratification for its own sake, is a notion difficult for some to accept. Why? If we assume good health and effective contraception, what could be the matter with a man and woman, or a couple of men and women, or a group engaging in recreational sex?

Unlike food, too much sex doesn't make people fat. Unlike drink or drugs, it does not distort behaviour and harm the body. There should be no restriction on enjoyment of pleasure. We should avoid pain and seek pleasure. Engaging in sex provides pleasure, but so does looking at other people engaged in sexual activity, or even just talking about sex.

Many people who rail against sex are often found to enjoy elicit sexual pleasures, such as Jim Baker and Swaggart. Many politicians are censured for being discovered in sexual pleasures. Just ask Edward Kennedy, Gary Hart, John Profumo and Greek Prime Minister Andreas Papandreou. As long as people do not abuse the welfare and dignity of others, it should be OK. Long ago married couples should have been educated in methods to enjoy sex so that they would have less reason to try elsewhere.

Children should see 'love-making' and intercourse as part of daily living just as the other animals do. Part of their education would be to learn how to make 'love-making' pleasurable. The idea is that young people should grow up without the hang-ups past generations have had. The prohibitions of the past only exaggerated the importance of sex and gave a false expectation. Prohibitions don't work. What is needed is education. Young people would probably experiment, but that is not bad.

Men will gradually realize that intercourse is not all that wonderful, and that they can enjoy the other parts of love-making, including masturbation by the partner. If he feels he must have intercourse, he should be allowed to have a prostitute.

Girls should be encouraged to stay virgins, because chastity is the best contraceptive. Chastity does not mean no sex. It just means 'outercourse' not 'intercourse'. They can still enjoy love-making.

Much of a woman's pleasure from intercourse is the joy of feeling wanted, the joy of being able to give something that a man so desperately wants. It is wrong to believe that without the release of sex, she will become a frustrated, bitter, cruel, dried-up envious old stick.

HUMAN BODIES SHOULD BE IMPROVED

It has taken over a million years for us to develop to the point we are at today, but we are still not the best. In fact we don't even know what would be best. The fact that nam became an upright animal, does not mean that upright is the best possible. It merely means that there were enough good features to let that arrangement survive. We don't know how much of our actions and thoughts are programmed into us by our genes, and how much is determined by our environment and experiences. But we know that our brain, with the help of the Unified Life Theory, is the key to finding a happier, better life.

Humans do many things because we are genetically programmed to want to. Our desire to have someone acknowledge us, by saying 'hello' as we pass, is similar to a dog's programme to wag its tail when happy.

'Base animal behaviour' and 'the lowest animal instinct' are expressions to indicate undesirable actions. However, animal instincts and behaviour are not base, they are what got us to where we are. They are normal for all animals including humans. Most animals have to kill to eat, but some have developed a socialization where they don't consider their own kind an enemy to be killed off. However, many do not, including the lion that sometimes eats young cubs, or a newly hatched bird that pushes the unhatched egg out of the nest.

Humans are, to a large extent, socialized to not kill each other, but it doesn't take much to over-ride this conditioning, as seen in our many historical wars, and the German genocide of Jews. In the animal world there is no right or wrong. Nothing is right or wrong, but thinking makes it so. There is no cruelty in the natural world, only reality. Predators are not mean, just hungry. Prey animals are not innocent, just intent on survival.

Unlike other animals, humans have brains and hands that permit us to change things to our advantage. If we don't have enough water in one location, we pipe it in from another. If we can't grow food in one area, we grow it in other places. If our arteries are clogged, our doctors can do a multiple heart by-pass. We use oil and electricity to move things and ourselves about. We construct buildings to keep us out of the weather.

'Natural selection' helped all animal species adopt to changing conditions and propagate the healthy and maybe the most intelligent. The offspring that were defective would die off, so the bad genes would not be continued. The strong and healthy males impregnated most of the females. There was definitely a selection going on that brought out the best for the changing conditions.

Evolution of a species does not proceed in any direction or toward some form of final perfection. The elephant and the manatee descended from the same ancestral stock, which shows that mutations can end up going in many directions.

Natural selection alters some species and eliminates others, and this goes on forever. Today it does not apply so much to humans, because almost everyone finds a mate, and the best don't necessarily have the most offspring. Therefore, there is no selection for good.

Our brain has made it possible to devise ways to keep even the sickly and malformed alive, and all types are having offspring to pass on good and bad genes. Humans are changing in ways that might lead to extinction if we allow natural selection to continue. In order to develop a being more suited to the present and future, we must initiate selective breeding in order to change the brain and body and our genetic programming.

For those born with physical handicaps, brain defects, or debilitating diseases, life is not likely to be nearly as enjoyable as for those without problems. The purpose in life is to try to enjoy life, so it only makes sense that we should try to bring into this world only those genes that have some hope of producing a reasonably happy individual. That means some form of selection to improve the human race.

In twentieth-century North America, the selection has been made mostly by 'love', but this basis of selection makes no attempt to eliminate the poor risks. Selection should now be on the basis of the best genes. What constitutes the best genes will vary with all our different races and groups, and this is good, but it should try to eliminate Down's syndrome, hepatitis, sickle cell anaemia, cystic fibrosis, haemophilia, muscular dystrophy, etc.

Eugenics is the study of the laws of heredity and how to use our knowledge so that future generations do not inherit the flaws of their ancestors. The knowledge gained from these studies should be widely publicized, and people encouraged to select their breeding partners so that offspring will be free of obvious problems. Eugenic ideas should not be used to justify laws authorizing involuntary sterilization of the mentally handicapped or regulations to try and prevent men and women with unhealthy family histories from having offspring. Emphasis should be on education and persuasion.

Better breeding would save our society money and improve the quality of life. Genetic engineering, including in-vitro fertilization, sperm banks, gene-splicing, and genetic screening, can be used to evolve desired traits. Reproductive technology has recently suggested that we may be able to clone humans from adult tissue cells (no need for a man's sperm). Go ahead. Send in the clones. It should not create any significant problems, because we are not trying to breed a race of thoroughbreds.

It used to be that we were proud of and interested in our ancestors. Who they were, where they were and what they did were important. Future generations will also be interested in their 'roots' as far as their gene characteristics are concerned. We breed plants and animals to produce a better variety. Why should we not do the same for humans? We should all have a registered pedigree.

Owls' eyes and many animals that prowl at night have evolved not only to be sensitive to so-called visible light, but also to the lower frequencies so that they can see at night. Humans have evolved to see in the visible light frequency rays. As far as we know, this was done by breeding, giving more success to those who were best at seeing in daylight. This type of reference is supposed to convince you that human characteristics and physical features can be altered, either by selective breeding or genetic engineering.

Another example of selective breeding is to raise fruit flies with 4 wings instead of 2 or with 12 legs instead of 6. Also, by selective breeding over a 100 year period, a 75 lb miniature horse, 27 inches at the shoulder, has been produced starting with a large horse measuring 6 feet at the shoulder.

White skinned people should have children with black skin in order to reduce the white nam's curse of skin cancer. To improve our bodies we should improve a liver that can't clear cholesterol from the blood stream; a system that allows cholesterol to block the flow of blood in arteries, causing heart attacks and strokes; a system that allows cancer cells to grow; males, so they would be less aggressive. We could easily get rid of baldness, wisdom teeth and hair on the face.

It is important to realize that we cannot rely on evolutionary forces of natural selection to free our race of unwanted characteristics, because the symptoms of damage occur late in life, after our child-bearing years are over. If we select a mate who, unknown at the time, will later develop bad features, the children will be born carrying the bad genes. Therefore, we can't rely on the selection of one's mate if we don't know hei's weaknesses while so young.

We must either use our brains to educate against mate selection without investigating the medical history of parents, or use our brains to engineer genetic changes to produce a better body. Humans can be crafted by genetic engineering. We are already having some success with a gene therapy that will lower the cholesterol concentrations in a patient's blood. A breast cancer gene has been isolated, and a blood test will be available to detect its presence.

Women can work at making their bodies stronger so that they will not be readily molested and can more readily cope with the physical demands of a male world. Women will ultimately want to be stronger just to feel safer in cases where extra strength could get them out of trouble, such as when they are trapped in a burning building and want to climb out of a window.

Women can do a great deal to counteract their genetic programming, but there is a limit to what can be done with their present bodies. If you want future women to be as strong as men, you have to start now with selective breeding. It will take many generations, but it can be done. Women could also be a major factor in genetically changing the male mind and body.

The female brain has kept pace with the male brain even though it would seem that in ancient times females were not in a position to use their brains as much as men. This could be a genetic thing that just happened, but women, more and more, are realizing that they need not be the submissive, child-bearing, supportive creature that past history programmed them to be. Maybe the meek shall inherit the earth, but don't count on it.

Today, women know they have the brain power to control their own lives and obtain more happiness. Women should see themselves not as victims, but as masters of their fate, and quite capable of controlling their professional, personal and sexual lives. They know they can compete with men in all but the more physical pursuits. Even this they could change if the more physical women bore more of the children, or if baby-makers used their eggs.

Up until recently one of a man's greatest desires was to carry on the family name by having sons. Male children were a man's hope for immortality. We live on through our genes in our children and grandchildren. Your blood is of my blood. Sons were given inheritances, not the wives. How did this come about? Probably because of the example set by the kings and the upper-class, where wives were mainly for beauty and sex and to bear children. Males were to carry on the family name. A wife was not a descendant of her husband, so she was not in line to inherit.

Kings and the upper-class had money and many slaves or servants, and therefore lived in a grand style. The upper-class had servants to make beautiful meals, wash the dishes, wash and iron the clothes, make the beds, clean and dust large spacious homes, and take care of a large number of children. Therefore, the other people thought of leisure, and not work, as the most wonderful life and tried very hard to live like the upper crust, even though they had no money. The men were probably the ones to insist that the wife do all these things that the servants did for the Royals. Today many people look on this as not worth the time and effort.

If our brains finally convince us that we should derive a great deal of happiness, knowing that we were doing something beneficial so that future generations could have a happier life, then we would try to change genetically the human body. Women will only have children if they and their mate have many of the desired genes. Inter-racial unions will also produce a good variety of humans. This should not be regulated by governments, but should be encouraged.

The greatest changes will be in the shape and strength of the human female body. The smooth skin and fine features will probably remain, but body strength and shape will be the target. The wide hips, that produce the wiggle which makes for poor athletic ability, would be discouraged. Melon-size breasts, or larger, are a great handicap for any sports activity, such as tennis.

Female bodies are not beautiful in most cases, and not many women have attractive breasts (breasts would have a better shape if women held their shoulders back), so they wear a brassière to reshape and fool the poor male.

Many animals have little evidence of breasts behind the nipples, and yet are successful feeders. Women with small breasts can be just as successful at feeding as large-breasted women. Even now, only half of women breast-feed their babies, so women don't need breasts, and the size could be genetically changed.

Male fruit bats in Malaysia have mammary glands that produce milk. We don't know if this is genetic or because of something they eat. We also know that certain human males have breasts that produce milk, so by genetic engineering we should be able to do all sorts of good things for both the male and female body.

In some animal species the female is as strong or stronger than the male. Here are a few examples. The female spotted hyenas, even the lowest ranking, are larger, more aggressive and dominant over the males. They even have genitalia closely resembling that of a male. The female bee does all the work and defends the nest. The male bees (there are few in number) have only one job, to mate with the queen. After mating, the male dies. Female bears are just as strong as the males. Female hawks are larger than the male. Lionesses do most of the hunting and killing (but the male is allowed to eat first). The female anaconda is three to five times larger than the male, and the female bonobo ape is stronger and dominates the male.

In the 1700s the King of the African nation called Dahomey had a regiment of warriors called the Ahosi, the most feared on the continent. They were his wives. This is solid evidence to indicate that, by genetic engineering, the human female can be changed.

There are many ways for animals to conceive, and just as many ways to give birth, so if the human female becomes dominant, she might genetically change the male to carry the foetus. This is already true among the seahorses where the male is the one to become pregnant. Who knows, someday each human society group may have only one queen, just like the bees.

Already it is possible to select sperm of the desired sex and have it implanted into the mother. Some say this is bad, because we could end up with nothing but male babies. That might not be so bad, but it's unlikely to happen, because people are so different, but if bees and ants and fish can do it, it might be a smart idea for humans to try.

One chap ran every day for many years and was never able to run the mile in less than 7 minutes. Long distance runners run faster than that for 25 miles. We should improve our human lung capabilities by selective breeding. This has already happened in one society where female pearl divers have developed lungs that allow them to go down 60 feet.

A woman's hymen is probably like an appendix. There seems to be no reason for them to have been genetically developed, but a woman's hymen is a detriment to her anticipation of sexual pleasure. This is another feature that could be eliminated by proper selection.

A woman who feels she must have the experience of being pregnant, and giving birth, yet fears passing on defective genes, would be encouraged to have a desired-male sperm, combined with a desired-female egg, implanted into her womb. This is in-vitro (sometimes called test-tube) fertilization. A woman with some of the desired characteristics could pass them on without even having to go through childbirth herself.

People who were really interested in improving the female's lot in the future, would promote the idea of selective breeding either by intercourse or by other newer means. Genetic engineering may someday make it possible directly to influence evolution by selecting the mutations desired. Have no fear that this could result in robot-like people who look alike. We people have such a variety of likes and dislikes, and variety is the spice of life.

Over the last century the role of men in our society has not changed very much. The role of women, on the other hand, has changed considerably. They got the vote, and they are getting equal rights at work, equal rights in marriage, equal rights as far as their children are concerned, equal rights to keep their name, equal rights to control their intercourse activity and the right to have an abortion.

The next big change will be when women decide to take charge and control the quantity and quality of our population. They are the ones who influence evolution, because they decide who the fathers will be. They are nature's gate keepers. They are the ones to carry a child through its development in the womb with all the pain, suffering and discomfort this entails. They are the ones to go through the pain and suffering of the birth.

The babies come out of the mother's bodies and should be theirs and theirs alone. The only part of the child that comes from the father is that one tiny sperm that starts things off. All the rest is up to the woman. A man doesn't even know for sure that it is his sperm that started this baby. Men should have no say concerning the child, unless the mother delegates that authority. She should select a first name for the baby (the second name would probably be the last name of the father if she knows the father's name), and the last name would be the same as the mother's last name.

If a man pays a woman to have a baby with his sperm and her egg, or a purchased egg, then the baby would be his and the mother would have no say concerning the child.

CENSORSHIP NEVER WORKS

Many animals live in groups, especially mammals, and other groups are considered enemies to be kept out of the home territory. So it is not surprising that humans retained this trait. Most of the wars during the past centuries have been between one ethnic group and another. Genghis Khan, the Turks, the Romans, Hitler and the Japanese are examples. Today, we have fighting between Jews and Palestinians, Serbs and Croats, South African whites and the ANC, the Irish and the English.

In the old days, people were born, raised and lived all their lives in one community, and things could be kept the same century after century. However, when people started moving to different locations, towns and countries, the situation changed. Many in Great Britain wanted to keep the black people of the colonies from emigrating and settling in England. They wanted to keep their island pure white, English, Anglo-Saxon. Automatic rejection of what is not familiar is a primitive reflex, suited to living in a dangerous jungle, but ill-advised in a neighbourhood or country that seeks coherence.

We have inherited the desire to be with our own. It is a feeling of comfort and familiarity. It is right. It is God's will. The latest book by Miss Manners describes what is right or wrong. In many places censorship and prohibition laws were passed to try to keep the 'others' out, or to make the other people conduct themselves according to a standard. But even if a large majority of the people want a certain way of life to be the only way of life around them, they should not pass laws to try to regulate everyone into one way of life.

You might as well get used to divergent wants and desires. In fact you should try some of the new ideas. You might find that you can enjoy them too. Sometimes it is time to consider 'sacrificing your Queen'.

In most large North American cities the Chinese, Italians, Philippinos, French, blacks and many other ethnic, religious, and linguistic groups live in their separate areas. This is a friendlier, less stressful arrangement for them. We should not try to prevent other people living the way they want to live. There should be no laws against freedom of expression. It is not natural to 'love your neighbours' when they are so different maybe in colour, race, religion, language and also in the way they dress, what they eat, how they act and what they do and say. Our brains have to over-ride our normal feelings and convince us that these other people are just as acceptable in their groups as we are in ours.

Why should we want our brains to overcome our animal instincts? Well, because it is logical, right and proper, democratic, liberal, but most of all, you should want to 'do unto others as you would want them to do for you'. The Unified Life Theory suggests that we must have one 'thou shall not', and that is we should not steal from or hurt or kill one another. All groups in our present societies would probably agree to that, and the only conflict would be in the degree of punishment for the various crimes.

Over the past years many laws have been passed to try to prevent people from doing and saying what they would like to do and say. The so-called Victorian era was full of 'thou shall nots', one of which was the beginning of censorship of the written word.

It probably came about because the nineteenth century maiden would teeter on the brink of fainting from loud noises, mice and any allusion to sex, or nudity. It was a man's duty to shield her from 'all that could pain or soil'.

In the twentieth century, people started to rebel against these restrictions. Women's bathing suits no longer had full skirts. Two-piece suits were in by 1950, and by 1970 those 'itsy-bitsy, teeny-weeny' little bikinis were standard. At every stage there was a hue and cry, saying we had gone far enough, and still today when we have already gone so far as to talk about condoms and penises, there are too many saying we have gone too far. There is no 'too far'.

We should not try to prevent people from saying or doing what they want to do, as long as it does not hurt others. Freedom of expression, and freedom of speech does not hurt anyone and should be a civil right. Everyone has the right to ee's type of pleasure as long as ee's lifestyle does not interfere with others' lifestyles too greatly.

Obscene is 'intending to cause sexual excitement or lust', but what's wrong with that if it gives pleasure? There should be no censorship, because it affects an adult's right to free choice. Blinkers are put on horses to keep them from seeing things that might tempt them to go in a direction other than that wanted by the driver. Adult censorship, in any form, amounts to blinkers being placed on you, and no matter what rationalization may be constructed around it, it is an attempt to control you. By its very nature, censorship is dictatorial. We should be saying the now famous phrase 'mad as hell, and not going to take it any more'. To hell with censorship.

Back in the 1930s and 1940s the Hayes Office would not allow movies with girls wearing two-piece bathing suits, and certain words were not allowed until Rhett Butler, in *Gone With The Wind,* said, 'I don't give a damn.' Now even the word penis is common, but some words are still not often used. One example was a word supposedly used on court documents in early England to describe rape, a charge that may have been fairly common in those days. Officially it was called For Unlawful Carnal Knowledge. The words were often shortened to just the first letters of each word, and thus in themselves became used as a word.

People today who are in favour of some censorship would not suggest we go back to the old ways, but they haven't yet realized that the censorship they want today will be as obsolete as the old restrictions. They are fighting a losing battle, because ultimately people will demand freedom.

The zealots who mistakenly believe that less erotica and less violence on TV will result in less promiscuity and less mayhem and fewer murders, are the direct descendants of the respectable people who banned *Madame Bovary* and *Lady Chatterley's Lover*.

The idea of censorship is archaic and pompous. There should be no person or group, even government, who has the right to abuse your freedom to read or view anything. If anyone would be offended, they shouldn't go to that movie, or they shouldn't turn on that TV programme. Producers only produce what people will watch. If audiences don't watch it, the producers won't show that stuff.

PORNOGRAPHY AND OBSCENITY

There should be no laws prohibiting pornography or obscenity. Where censorship laws have been eliminated, sex crimes have fallen, probably because material can be found easily enough for those in need to find release.

We should eliminate police 'Morality Squads' (think of the money that would be saved) because it is monstrous to send anyone to prison for something which you cannot prove is harmful. Time and money should be spent on sex education of the young, so they won't grow up having to look for the answers to the mysteries of sex.

Puritans and censors have apparently been taught that sex is something to be afraid of. They don't want sex to be a permissible subject. They cannot really accept the simple realities of life, and the sight of the human body means sex to them, and sex gives them the horrors.

The average age of porn customers is over 40, because the material appeals chiefly to hung-up relics of a more repressive time. Rather than crack down on their pathetic 'jollies' we should hope to create a society where real life is more attractive than their fantasy material.

There should not be any laws that require a judgement call. Normally, the burden of proof or guilt must fall on the prosecution to establish guilt beyond any reasonable doubt. In cases involving obscenity or pornography, the prosecutor simply assumes that the book or magazine is harmful without saying anything to prove it.

HOMOSEXUALS AND LESBIANS

We don't know how 'they' get to be like they are, whether it is genetic or from their upbringing and socialization. But it shouldn't matter that they are different than the vast majority of people. Many so-called 'straight' people have pretty kinky sexual desires and practices, such as whipping, cross-dressing, oral and rectal intercourse, weird positions, underwater sex and even sex with animals. What is so different with same-sex sex? Up until recently homosexuality was considered a gross and sinful thing, even though it was known to exist in the animal world. The other animals didn't seem to object and neither should we. If they enjoy it, let them. It doesn't hurt anyone else.

It is difficult for a heterosexual person to understand how a homosexual man would want to insert his penis into another man's rectum. For many, it would seem to be an unpleasant experience, as indicated by the story of the male rabbit that was out jumping on females. Bam-bam, 'thank you, mam', bam-bam, 'thank you, mam', and on to the next and bam-bam, 'Goddam, that you, Sam?' It would appear to be much more difficult, because a rectum is not easy to penetrate even when lubricated. Since being given an enema is never pleasant, it is difficult to understand the recipient's feelings. However, many find it pleasurable.

It is assumed that women, even with multiple orgasms, get less pleasure from intercourse than men. In fact, we assume that much of a woman's pleasure is the feeling of power, knowing that she can turn a man on and give him such pleasure. If her man does not give her pleasure, or if she has no man, she should consider another woman for sex.

As barriers gradually disappear, as they will, more and more women will find that a lesbian encounter will be more rewarding. You would think that a woman would much prefer a female's finger in her vagina, gently caressing her clitoris, than a man's penis which can mess her up with a tablespoonful of unwanted semen. And, most importantly, lesbians can have 100% AIDS protection by wearing a rubber glove just like the dentist or doctor.

A man likes to be with a pretty woman; the world would be a poorer place without beautiful women and delightful female voices. She makes him laugh, makes him feel important, is interesting to talk to, does such interesting things, shares the same interests, and is smart. A woman likes a man for the same reasons. But a man likes to be with a man for the same reasons, and a woman likes to be with a woman for the same reasons.

It's not surprising that women find many men sexually terrifying and physically hurtful and therefore turn to other women for emotional and physical comfort. Lesbians are not undermining the institution of marriage and family any more than the heterosexuals who are already showing that the nuclear family is not the best social arrangement. There should be no special laws promoting marriage or benefits supplied to married couples. We should be promoting an extended family concept, where homosexuals and lesbians and straight people would all be equal. We are animals and should not try to prevent people from doing what they would like to do.

PROSTITUTION

Laws against prostitution are still trying to prevent girls from 'selling their bodies'. Women sell their bodies in many ways. If they are beautiful or shapely they can make money as models. They can sell the speed of their fingers on a typewriter, the quality of their voice, their skill as a salesperson or a scientist. Already they are selling their bodies to make babies. It's probably better than prostitution. They used to sell their hair, and they should be allowed to sell their vaginas if they so choose.

Women should make use of their best assets. If they are good at the piano, basketball, flying, bridge, teaching, pleasing men sexually, tennis, acting, truck-driving, designing or supervising, they should do it if it brings in the most money and/or it gives the most pleasure.

Life isn't reasonable or just. You weren't born an ape, a humming bird, an autistic or a paraplegic, so you have to get along with what you've got. Men unconsciously see themselves as prostitutes, selling their bodies every day. The miner, the fire-fighter, the construction worker, the logger, the soldier, the meat-packer, the boxer all sacrifice their bodies for money. So in effect we all sell our bodies.

Both men and women strive hard to acquire a skill, or something that others will pay money for, so they can buy food, clothing, housing and pleasure. We go to school and college for years to acquire marketable skills. We must spend endless hours practising our skill in sports if we wish to make a living in professional sports.

How nice it is when we have savings in the bank or something of value that is always available, if times are tough, and we can't find desired employment. Most men have only their strong muscles to sell for lifting and shovelling, but women have their vaginas which are always in great demand. It is true that there is a danger of venereal disease and AIDS, but protection is available.

Women should not sell their vaginas cheaply. Girls soon learn that boys want to touch and feel and get into their bodies. This desire is strong and very compelling. Women have been using their vaginas to get what they want since the beginning of time. They tell men they can't have intercourse unless they promise marriage to take care of them for the rest of their lives. They tell the casting director that it can be had only if they get a part in the play. So why should their selling sex for money be outlawed? Who is kidding whom?

Prostitution was officially promoted in ancient Greece in order to protect the family. If prostitution were a legitimate service industry, the women who wanted to do this work would be in houses or buildings especially designed for this use and would be clean and attractive. Instead of using tax dollars to try and prevent prostitution, we should have people checking facilities to publish ratings for each establishment.

Laws against prostitution should be abolished. Just think of the tax money to be saved. Think of the advantage for the women. They wouldn't have to pay pimps and would not be walking the streets and getting into cars where there is so great a danger of being badly hurt or killed. We would have fewer children kid-napped for sex. We should not have laws to try to prevent consenting people doing what they want to do. Government should not be involved with what goes on in the bedrooms of the nation.

DRUGS

The use of drugs is as old as prostitution. People take drugs because they like the rush of pleasure, the high nirvana it gives. It will sweep away grave anxiety and physical anguish. Chemicals affect the endorphin transmitters in the brain and give us feelings of euphoria. Even bananas are supposed to reduce the bad PMS feeling. What we need to do is not outlaw drugs, but learn their effects and educate.

The use, marketing, processing and growing, gathering or mining of drugs should not be illegal. Tobacco, alcohol, marijuana, cocaine and heroin should all be as legal as glue and other common substances that can be sniffed, ingested or injected for special effects. Sure, most drugs are addictive, harmful and downright dangerous, but it is one's own body to do with as one sees fit.

We know that people are spending too much money on drugs when they don't have enough to feed their family properly. But [redacted] prohibition does not work. We should spend tax dollars to educate people about the dangers, and we should also make sure that people are aware of the purity and concentration of the product, as well as its being germ free.

The amount of tax dollars spent on prohibition is staggering, and the number of officers killed or hurt trying to prevent this trade is unjustifiable. Far more people suffer because of drugs being illegal than if drugs were legal. Just think of the number of offences committed by people who must get money to support their very expensive drug habit.

People are mugged and robbed and killed on the street. Numerous people are badly hurt or shot during house break-ins. Stores are held up for cash, and often the cashier is shot. Clients who don't pay up are badly roughed up by their dealers. Think of the problem and heart-thumping drama each user must go through in order to get ee's supply without being caught by the police.

Think of the people who are used to smuggle the drugs into your neighbourhood. All this because the price of drugs is so high and not easily obtained.

Drug lords make millions of dollars, because the sales prices can be kept artificially high. The prices are high because the cost of smuggling illegal drugs is huge, but the main reason is the profits made. Crime lords exist when there is a need for a strong organization to combat or work against the law. Take the laws away and you get rid of the lords. De-criminalizing drugs and making them available and inexpensive does not mean that we condone their use. It simply means we know that prohibition never works.

Many methods would be used to discourage drug use. For instance, selling drugs to athletes should not be illegal, but athletes found using drugs would not be allowed to compete in competitions. Drug-users found driving a car or involved in other activities where the public could be in danger would be in trouble with the law, just as alcohol-users are now.

Most young people will not get involved with substances when they are told of the dangers. Substances in the medicine cabinet marked POISON will be left alone. Peer pressure is strong and is considered the main cause of kids trying drugs, or doing something they know they shouldn't, so they must be taught how to resist. We must do a better job of convincing people that smoking and the taking of drugs and alcohol is dangerous.

Some people think a little alcohol is okay, but insist that a little drug-taking isn't. For some reason we don't consider alcohol itself to be evil. Instead we view its consumption as dangerous, and respond compassionately toward the individuals who become addicted. There is no thought of trying to outlaw it.

The reaction to someone using drugs is just the opposite. We rail against the drug, and say, 'If only we could stamp out the drugs, this tragedy would never have happened.' Well, for goodness sake, smarten up. Drugs will never be stamped out, no matter how much we spend in time, money and lives. We can't even keep drugs out of prisons.

The supply of drugs will always be made available by the drug lords as long as people are willing to pay the price. Drugs are very much like alcohol. There is no hope of prohibition being successful. There are too many people wanting the stuff. If that many want it, why should we try to deny them?

Just think of the number of people buying drugs. It seems there is a dealer on almost every corner, and for every dealer there have to be a hundred buyers. That's a lot of people. That's a lot of money. The political and economic impact of the trade in its illegitimate form is seen in the phenomenal funds generated by drug dealers, and the violence they commit to protect their interests, to say nothing of their corruption of government agencies.

Wouldn't you like to destroy the rich drug lords? All you have to do is remove the restrictive laws so that the price will fall to a fraction of today's price. Drugs, like crack, should be available in pill or capsule, with the contents guaranteed by government inspection. Simple, isn't it? Logical, isn't it? We shouldn't try to keep people from doing what they want to do.

CLOTHES OPTIONAL

We are born without clothes, and it is not logical to require clothing as we grow older. Animals don't have a problem with the fact that they can distinguish males from females. In warm climates, native tribes had no problem with both sexes without clothing. At the Olympic games in ancient Greece, contestants were all naked athletes. How it came about that both sexes were required to be fully clothed, even in bed, either by law or custom, is not really important.

The degree of covering up has changed back and forth over the centuries. The Victorian era was probably the time of most covering up except maybe the Muslim requirement for females to be completely covered except for the eyes. Women back then were required to keep their ankles and almost everything else covered, presumably so that men would not be stimulated to think about sex, or to think of women as sex objects.

As women gradually decided to become more active and to have fewer clothing restrictions, skirts got shorter and breasts became more visible. When they found that men's attitude did not change much, no better or worse, they went further until bikinis covered nipples and pubic hair, and yet a man's reaction was little changed. Today some girls go topless in public, and still it is obvious that men are no more stimulated than when women were completely covered.

Women know they are sex objects, and they know they can't change that. They have been telling men for some time now that they want to be desired and admired not only for sex but for their brains, their abilities in the working world and for their characteristics as worthwhile people. One way to reinforce this image is to be without clothing in the company of men, so that men will get used to the idea that nakedness is not a 'come-on' for sex. Women want men to know that the sex object isn't available unless a definite signal is given.

You should stop and analyze everything you do or don't do, and see if it is going to give you the most happiness. Spotlighting absurdities in our society is the first step toward eliminating them. If you act like all the others act, check and see if this is really logical or the best idea. Unfortunately too many humans are ruled by the social pressure of 'everyone does it, so it must be right' syndrome.

It is like tipping the <u>waitree</u>. Everyone does it. It is the custom. In the beginning there may have been a good reason for tipping. Some say that 'tip' comes from 'to insure promptness', but that would require tipping before service is started. Today we tip afterward, and we don't tip because we received good service. Even if the service is not good, we tip. Why? Because it is the custom, and everyone does it.

Tipping is a bribe. When we hear that you can't do business in Russia or China without paying bribes, we think that is dreadful. It's also discouraging that tips are not declared for tax purposes. This is as bad as paying a contractor in cash to get a lower price, knowing <u>ee</u> will not show your payment on <u>ee's</u> tax return.

Many don't admit it, but they tip to impress their dinner partners. They want to imply that they are big spenders. A tip of 10% used to be the accepted standard until too many people wanted to show their dinner partners that they not only tipped, but they tipped generously, like 15%. Gradually the rest of us switched to

15%, so we wouldn't be considered cheap. Many people, especially those eating alone, have quit tipping, and gradually the rest of us will do the same.

Some say the pay is very low, and waitrees deserve more, but if they were not getting tips, they would quickly demand more pay. There are many other people making the minimum wage, and we don't tip them, and we shouldn't. Those who worry about the pay being low might want to leave a 'calling card' so the waitree could show it to ee's boss to prove ee did not receive a tip of money. The card might read:

My TIP is SYE

To	See
Improve	Your
Pay	Employer

How silly and illogical is tipping, but it shows how people feel compelled to conform. The same is true of clothing to cover the body. There is no logical reason for it.

Some say nakedness is not attractive. Seeing a woman's pubic hair certainly can't be classed as seeing something ugly or unsightly; you can't see much else down there. The genitals of a naked man are much more obvious, but they are no more ugly than some ears, noses, beer-barrel tummies or fat ladies. We should not be required to cover up when it is hot and sweaty just because some people don't like the look of naked people.

Some say that nakedness is titillating and sexy, and this kind of arousal should not be all over the streets. But if you restrict public nudity to 'nude girlie shows', you are promoting the feeling that the female body is a sex object. If you want to change that, you should promote the idea of a 'clothes optional society'.

In every case where nakedness is normal, at nudist resorts, nude beaches, and in France and other European countries where there are many 'clothes optional' towns, you will find the naked body is no longer an incitement to sex. It's like cars. After you've seen people naked a few times the novelty wears off. Sure, if a new model comes out, you will look at it.

Maybe some day when nakedness is normal, it will become customary for a woman to greet another individual by taking ee's hand and bringing it to her breast, holding it there while the other gives a gentle squeeze. This would probably be a greeting more friendly than a handshake, more loving than a cheek kiss, and less loving than a lip kiss (and less germy too).

Some say nakedness should be reserved for a special occasion. Undressing your loved one is one of the more important methods of arousal. It is a tender loving act. However, you should not think that if you should see naked people on the beach or playing tennis, or just talking to each other, that you would no longer be turned on by the act of undressing your sex partner. This has not been the experience of nudists or couples who normally go to bed together without pyjamas. They will still enjoy the undressing preliminary when sex play begins. Nudity has a special place in the act of love, but nakedness also has a special place in the art of living.

It's interesting to realize that people get dressed to go to bed. This no doubt started when what one slept on and under was not good insulation. Now that homes are heated, mattresses and covers are warm, and heating blankets are available, there is no need for night-shirts or pyjamas, unless, of course, society has by now decreed that the body must be covered at all times. The only problem with sleeping nude is keeping your breath from tickling your arm when you are on your side. The solution is to cover your arm with the sheet or blanket or pillow.

Those who would allow nudity only in the marriage bed are trying to condemn so many to never seeing a naked body. Many a married man is seen at the 'nude girlie shows', because he sees his wife naked only in Braille under the covers. If we had public nudity, we would have less need of pornographic magazines, obscene literature, burlesque shows and flashers.

Developing a naturalness towards the naked body will be the beginning of a healthy attitude towards sex. Nakedness in sports, on the beach, or working in the yard would be one of the best possible kinds of sex education for children and young people.

They would not be pushed into clandestine sex by the 'you show me yours, and I'll show you mine' society. It is every child's inalienable right to know what the human body looks like and to be comfortable with it. Ignorance is not bliss. It's dangerous. When we deliberately keep our youngsters in ignorance, thinking we are protecting them, we do them harm. When we are silent because of our discomfort, we fail them.

It is no doubt true that when the first nudist appears publicly, it would be distracting, but so was the first girl to wear a mini-skirt to the office. If the legal restrictions were removed, only a few would take advantage of it to start with, because of social pressures. (You continue to wear a tie to work, but there is no law to say that you must.)

Having clothes on when you are hot is most uncomfortable and annoying and should not be required. A country's constitution that guarantees freedom of expression should, under that heading, automatically guarantee freedom from clothing restrictions.

We should not have laws with penalties concerning things some people don't like. You wouldn't want laws against farting or burping in public, (in some societies, burping after a meal is a sign of having had a good meal). 'It's better to burp and feel the shame than not to burp and feel the pain.' You might end up with 'no smoking, no farting, no burping' sections in restaurants.

Nudists should have a booth at the Sportsnam Show. Skinny-dippers should be out demanding 'clothes optional beaches'. Nudists should come out of the closet and tell their friends and neighbours about the enjoyable lifestyle. There are huge numbers of nudists, so isn't it time to get some publicity in the press, on radio and on TV?

Nudists are a group who have been unjustly treated, just like the black Americans were until the time was right and they said 'no' to going to the back of the bus. Just like gays who were unjustly treated until the time was right and they came out of the closet. We should not try to prevent people from doing what they would like to do.

GAMBLING

Let us think of gambling not as a game of chance to win money, but of taking chances where you could win or lose. With that definition we can agree that all animals, including ancient nam and all our ancestors, were chance-takers to some degree. All the explorers were gamblers. Columbus risked all and won. Many of the searchers for the North West Passage failed. Some have tried to climb the highest mountain and failed. Today we still hear of people who have taken a chance and won or lost.

How many have put all their savings into starting a business only to have it fail, but some have won and gone on to great success. In other words, gambling is normal. People decide to take a chance when they calculate that their chances of winning are well above 50%, but this is not true for people who bet at bingo, blackjack, roulette and the many types of lotteries.

The difference is that the stakes are not usually very high, so that losing is no deal. In fact the gamblers expect to lose, but they keep playing because if they do win, it can often be a large amount. Some consider gambling an investment. A small amount each week may turn into a bonanza.

In some cases, the addictive gambler spends so much time and money that people relying on hei are severely affected. Many people who don't gamble feel that there should be a law against gambling in order to prevent the bread-winner of the family from losing too much money. But the family as a social institution is not the best, so should not be protected. Gambling is only one of so many things that could cause the breakdown of a family. There is no point in trying to prop up a dying institution. We should not try to prevent people from doing what they would like to do and will do regardless of any laws.

It is not our job to restrict gambling by any means other than education and information. It would help a great deal if the gambler knew what the probabilities of winning were. If they knew how much by way of expenses and profits were taken out before any pay-out, they might think twice about their chances.

Gambling has come a long way from prohibition days, but it's still not wide open. Governments are now the ones making money, lots of money, from what used to be illegal.

To their infinite credit, the Chinese make no bones about the fact that they adore gambling. If there are two birds on a fence, the Chinese saying goes, there will also be two people eager to bet on which one flies away first.

An argument against gambling is that the money could be spent on food and clothing for the family. But the same is true of many activities. With that argument, we should not have baseball stadia. The money spent could better have been used to feed or clothe the children. There is no point in trying to control how a person spends ee's money.

Many people still can't see that all these gradual changes are leading to the ultimate complete relaxation of restrictive laws. They still feel they must have some restrictions, but it's a lost cause. Freedom will come, but it should be sooner rather than later.

KILLING IS SOMETIMES OK

It is assumed that our ancestors did not consider life to be precious. They were predators. They killed animals for food and killed their human enemies. This is probably a genetic thing that is still with us today. This genetic program apparently made our type of human successful enough to prosper. All through our recorded history we have done a lot of killing and we are now the most lethal predator. *Homo sapiens* murders 200,000 of its own species each year, not including the millions killed in car accidents, suicides, and war. Today we don't have to be afraid of the beast in the field, we must worry about the beast in nam.

When modern nam went looking for aboriginal nam in Samoa and New Guinea, they found tribes of war-like people who were forever going off and killing neighbouring people. Their boys did not become men until they had killed, and in some cases they sacrificed a daughter to their gods.

If it was a means of our success back then, how can we say it is bad? Possibly it is because in the society that we have developed, our brains now tell us that other people have as much right to life as we do. The only reason people will not kill is when their brains tell them that life would be so much more pleasant if one did not have to be afraid; if one didn't have to be on guard all the time. It would be nice to walk the streets and live life without fear of attack. If we want a society where killing is not acceptable, and if we are a majority, we should proclaim that human life is a most precious thing, and this should be part of our Unified Life moral code. This grows out of our own thinking and not from some higher authority such as God.

However, we no longer have to feel that life should be maintained, saved, continued no matter what the cost; that every living person, no matter how unsocial, must be helped to be redeemed; that 'thou shall not kill' must be adhered to, because we should not play God. Without all these impediments we are left with the simpler problem of what is best for our society.

Reverence for life should mean that we wish to preserve life, but not at all costs. At present, even most of those who argue against taking life, agree that there is a limit beyond which it is not in the interest of the individual or society to preserve a life.

One example of this is when a person is a threat to society, such as a serial killer, or if a person is threatening another person's life. Another is aborting or killing an unborn baby when it threatens the life of the mother, or if the unborn baby is known to be abnormal. In other words, we have already agreed that there are limits purely for the benefit of society, and to avoid a person having a poor quality of life. The factors governing when killing is acceptable depend on how much society is willing to put up with.

DEATH PENALTY

We do not 'degrade' or 'brutalize' our society when we put to death people who break certain laws, if death is considered a proper penalty. An armed robber who kills would lose his normal right to life. This is not an 'eye for an eye', but a reasonable decision for society. The death penalty is not revenge, it is justice and economical. We should kill for the betterment of our society in such circumstances as abortion; the death penalty for many crimes; euthanasia; vivisection.

Unauthorized killing or hurting is detrimental to the good of our society and therefore should not be allowed. Instead of the 'sanctity of life' it is the 'quality of life' that should be a dominant factor for our society. With this as a basis, we would have a better guide to the question of capital punishment which should be acceptable under certain conditions. Keeping a person in prison for the rest of ee's life is not adding 'quality of life' for the tax-payer, who must work hard and long to make enough money to keep the person in prison at a cost that is more than the average worker's annual salary.

Five people are floating in a metal tub after an accident at sea. If a sixth tries to get in, the vessel would sink. Should the sixth be kept out? Yes, because the sixth would be in the same condition if the tub sank.

Take another situation where six people are obviously going to die, but if there were only five, all five would survive. Should one be killed to save five? Our new moral rule says not to kill, so that should be a 'no-no'. However, it would be hoped that one would decide to give up ee's life to save the others. It would be an honour to allow others to live.

ABORTION

There is a similarity between the arguments for and against capital punishment and the arguments for and against abortion. People who are against abortion are mostly those who believe in the soul, and that humans are put here for a purpose.

Well, this leads to an awful lot of problems as to when a foetus is a human being with a soul. One religious group says it is when the sperm has penetrated the egg. Another group says it is in about the 24th week when the cortex of the brain starts to send brain waves.

The Unified Life Theory does not leave you with this problem, because logic leads you to a better understanding. Every time our body produces a sperm or an egg, it is producing a life-form. A sperm wiggles and swims, so it must have something like a muscle. It must have a rudimentary brain, because it heads right for the egg, and if it doesn't get in at one point it tries another. Both egg and sperm are living things that have a certain lifespan. Life is just matter in a peculiar form. An egg, not fertilized, is matter that gets transformed into other substances, maybe part of another egg eventually.

Our society has no reason to worry about getting rid of something like 400,000 eggs which one woman makes in her ovaries in her lifetime, or getting rid of excess male sperm each time a male has an orgasm. It's like having a goitre removed. If it's not wanted, get rid of it.

We need laws relating to the 'rights of the individual' so governments will not imprison people if they disagree with the government's policies, for instance. This, however, does not apply to the unborn foetus, because it is not yet a person.

A fertilized egg grows into a foetus as part of the mother. A foetus is not a separate human being with a 'right to life' until after the umbilical cord is cut and the baby is out of the mother, breathing on its own. Only then should we talk about its 'sanctity of life'.

Women should not have to continue with a pregnancy conceived by rape, or ones not wanted for whatever reason. The Unified Life Theory suggests we no longer have to weigh the evidence to decide whether a birth would be detrimental to the woman's health or life; consider her state of mental health to make a decision; worry that she might be sorry that the child was aborted; try and decide when a foetus is a human person with a soul. If a woman wants an abortion, she should have one, and the male should have no say in the matter.

Hitler's mother and Einstein's mother both considered having an abortion. We certainly would have been better off without Hitler, but if Einstein had been aborted, the theory of relativity might have been longer in coming. But so what? Think of all the other scientists who didn't get born.

A recent TV ad has a mother, who did not have the abortion she had contemplated, saying 'I can't imagine life without little Jimmy.' If she had had the abortion and later decided to have a baby, it would not have been Jimmy, true, but she is forgetting all of the other eggs she will produce which will not be impregnated to become little Jimmies. What about them? Don't they have the right to be born too? Of course not. Life is only important to the individual. To the rest of society, life is only important according to the way it fits in with the community. Once a person or society logically decides that we are animals, then it would be agreed that preserving life is only a good idea if it would be good for our society. Ending a life that is not desirable should be no big deal.

There is no God-given 'right' and 'wrong'. Wrong is what our society decides is wrong, and that may only be by a bare majority.

So abortion cannot be called wrong if it is best for our society (not even if the Pope says it's wrong).

Should abortions be used to avoid births of inferior quality? China is advising pregnant women, who have been diagnosed as having certain infectious diseases or an abnormal foetus, to have an abortion. In North America we should also encourage women to have an abortion under these conditions, because an abnormal child will have so much less of a chance to have a normal or enjoyable life. Even if the defect is minor, it might be best to abort and try again for a better one.

The 'right-to-life' people and advocates for the disabled are appalled at this suggestion. 'If someone had made that decision about the 43 million Americans who were born disabled, they wouldn't be here today.' But if those 43 million had been aborted, and if the couple tried again, society would have 43 million people who would be a lot happier, more productive, and require far less money, time and care.

No one can say that one woman's egg has more right to life than any other of her eggs. One mother taking care of a Down's syndrome son said it was 'the most enriching experience of my life.' That's good, but she would have been happier if he had been aborted and another normal child raised.

The right-to-life philosophy is not reasonable, because it is trying to protect only one kind of life. If it wanted to protect all life, it would have all the eggs in each human female, plus the sperm in each male, brought to successful human life. That philosophy isn't workable so it's not reasonable.

More of our time and money should be spent promoting abstinence and contraception devices (including the RU-486 pill) in order to reduce the number of abortions.

SUICIDE

All animals and insects instinctively try to survive, and do all manner of things to avoid being killed. Some animals with their leg caught in a trap will gnaw away at their leg until it is cut off, and they are free to hobble away. That must be a painful procedure, but the desire to stay alive is strong. It must be a genetic thing that is in all of us. In the beginning, any animal not having that built-in genetic desire to live would perish, and its genes would not be passed on.

The only animals known to commit suicide are humans. Humans do seem to have the genetic program that makes them want to stay alive, however, they also have a most unique brain which can overcome genetic programming on occasion. Humans do have a great desire to stay alive, but if life becomes too painful or too distressing in many cases they will want to die rather than continue with the suffering.

Some people talk about the sanctity of life. They say all humans are made in the image of God, and the act of suicide, therefore, is deicide, the killing of a God. 'Thou shall not kill' applies to oneself as well as others, thus precluding suicide as well as any assistance in suicide. Life should not be valued in terms of the absence of pain, but in terms of holiness.

People who think this way will suffer to stay alive in order not to die before it is God's will. It also allows them to put themselves into situations where the possibility of their death is great, such as the wartime Japanese kamikaze pilots, and the Islamic Jihad terrorists, who believed their suicide mission was God's will, and that their souls would forever live with God.

These people are not likely to commit suicide, nor are they likely to request that they be helped to end their lives (assisted suicide) even if they are suffering great pain. If it is their belief, they are free to live that way, but they have no right to impose the rules of their beliefs on other people.

It is illogical to have laws concerning suicide, because we can't prevent a person from ending <u>ee's</u> life by jumping off a bridge, shooting <u>eeself</u>, hanging, or by any number of horrendous acts. In other words, it should not be against the law to help someone self-destruct, and certainly there should not be a suicide law where you are punished if you do not commit the 'offence' successfully. How silly.

'If it weren't for the dying, I'd wish I were dead.' 'Life is just a bowl of cherries, mostly pits.' 'We didn't ask to be born, so if we don't like life, why not get out.' 'Whose life is it anyway?' Means should be available to die with dignity.

People should be able to do with their lives as they wish. If they are thinking of suicide, they are no doubt in some degree of pain or suffering or depression. Certainly they should also consider the effect their death would have on other people. There may be someone or something or many who depend on them or are better off because of them. The amount of time, effort, and money spent on their upbringing and education should also be considered. It's not fair to their society for them to waste all that, unless the painful situation is too traumatic and not surmountable. We should remember that suffering for nothing is not known in the animal world, and should not be known in ours.

ASSISTED SUICIDE

We can't stop people from taking their own lives if they are physically able. So why should we stop people from having an assisted suicide just because they are not able to do it themselves?

Humans are like machines. They wear out, and in many cases should be scrapped. The wearing-out process is most painful. Pain is a common part of the human experience, and in most instances is the only warning we get that something is wrong, but there is no logical reason we shouldn't stop the pain if we can, once we get the message.

Pain comes in many forms, and physical pain is not necessarily the worst. Depression, and loneliness can be devastating to some people, and our society should have help available for this type of pain as well as the physical pain. Counselling and palliative care should be available, but when a person decides that ee has had enough, assisted suicide should also be available.

Many terminally ill people do not want a lingering death. They want to decide for themselves how much is enough and when to leave. For those who freely and competently ask for it, there should be a dignified and painless way out, including the pulling of the plug if they are on life-support.

The Catholic Church says it is permissible to discontinue medical support of the dying, but causing death is murder. How silly a dividing line. We shoot horses, don't we, to save them pain and suffering? We should do the same for humans, only there is a difference. The horse can't tell us whether ee would prefer to bear the pain, in order to continue living, but humans can. Therefore assisted suicide should be available when requested.

Medical doctors would not *have* to help people die, but doctor-assisted suicides would most likely be requested, because doctors have the skill, knowledge, compassion and facilities to accomplish the results painlessly. When assisted suicide is available it gives us a sense of control and asserts our individual rights. Most would want their loved ones around. They need that love, but in any case, they do not have to precipitate their own end if they don't want to. They have control. They don't have to take the prick of the needle unless they want to.

Anyone should be allowed to assist in a suicide, but there should be some approval procedure for the assistant to follow. Primarily this should consist of making sure that the person wanting to end ee's life is quite happy and desirous of having that individual assist in ee's quitting this life. Preferably the assistant should have a written statement and a witness as evidence that ee is not a murderer.

There should be no regulation or law requiring a specific number of doctors to certify that the person is terminally ill, or that ee has less than a certain number of months to live. There need not be any specific safeguards to protect the so-called vulnerable, frail and economically disadvantaged.

Sure, we should try to dissuade them from suicide, and offer assistance where feasible to alleviate their problem, but if a person can't wait, that is ee's nature, and we should not demand that ee go against ee's nature. They should have the final say. There should be no laws relating to assisted suicide. All we need are the existing laws relating to murder, on the assumption that, if permission is given, the death cannot come under the heading of murder.

Many people in nursing homes have nothing to live for, but the idea of suicide does not enter their minds, because life is dear to them. But there are those who would choose to end their lives, if doing so was acceptable, accessible and painless.

Humans have the ability to foresee, to contemplate, and potentially control their own death. This is one of the qualities that show us to be different from all other animals. Rather than degenerating helplessly, the ill person, unlike other animals, can choose the timing, the setting and the circumstances of death. Ee may prepare friends and family for the end; make reasonable provisions for the welfare of others; complete worldly duties; and take leave of loved ones in a dignified manner.

Yes, we would have many more assisted suicides if it were legal, but that would be to reduce the pain and suffering so many people are presently going through. The Unified Life Theory would certainly approve the reduction of pain and suffering for so many people. Our young would be aware of this attitude toward life, but if emphasis is placed on the idea of reducing the pain of living, and if they knew that help would be available to get them out of the situation, there would not be an increase in suicides. In fact they would probably be reduced.

This is not a devaluation of human life. It merely allows people who rationally anticipate a life of misery to choose death with dignity. Those who are old and sick and miserable might think of death as a way to make room for children. Like the terminally ill in pre-modern Eskimo society, who walk off into the cold, today's patients might well act out of consideration and compassion for their loved ones. We are animals. We live and die. Only the truth shall set us free.

For the sun will rise, and the moon will set
And you learn how to settle for what you get.
It will all go on if we're here or not.
So, who cares? So what.
So, who cares? So what.

EUTHANASIA

Assisted suicide assumes the consent of the person. Euthanasia, in this discussion, assumes the mercy killing of a person who is unable to give consent at the time. If the consenting person has made a 'living will', voluntarily and intentionally requesting assistance in death, then ee's wishes should be honoured. If there is no 'living will', then the decision should be left up to doctors, relatives and friends to decide what that person would want done, according to things ee has said earlier.

The legal system could be set up to allow a judge or a jury to hear evidence and make a decision to avoid any charges of murder. The sanctity and quantity of life should not prevail over quality of life unless the patient has so indicated in the past.

ANIMALS

Should we kill animals, or use animals? Certainly in the animal world predators kill all the time, every day, in every way. Animals use other animals: sucker fish ride around on larger fish; wasps use live caterpillars in which to lay their eggs. Dominant animals kill lesser animals. There is no right and wrong in this. This is animal behaviour. There is no so-called moral judgement to be made. This is the way it is and was for animals, and we are animals.

The difference with humans is that our brain tells us that we can over-ride our genetic programming if we feel it is best for our group. Our brains will tell us that we should not kill other animals any more than we should destroy plants without good reason, because plants and animals have as much right to life as we do.

Should we eat meat knowing the pain and suffering of the animals? We are animals who like to eat meat. If we didn't have this special brain, we would not think about the pain that our prey go through. Other animals don't think about it. This is evident when we see the lion not bothering to kill the deer before it starts to tear chunks of flesh from its hind quarters or when we see our cat carrying a live mouse in its mouth.

The Unified Life Theory moral rule will be decided by the majority, and it probably will be that we should not kill or hurt unless there is a good enough reason for it. Feeding ourselves is a good reason, as long as the animal is not endangered, and not hurt unnecessarily. The same argument applies to using animals in medical or scientific experiments or for teaching.

We should always cause as little pain as possible to trap

animals. But where the product is a fur coat or some useful or pleasurable item, there may come a time when humans will decide to stop killing particularly if the animal is endangered. We don't think much about what animals are like when we kill them for food or leather, or experiment on them or use them as work animals. We resist thinking of them as intelligent or sensitive, but they are, and we should do what we can to avoid pain.

People are beginning to realize that our expanding population is causing all kinds of animals and insects to disappear, and this is not good for the future well-being of humans. There is no reason to worry about stepping on an ant, crushing a cockroach, swatting a fly, killing a pigeon that is messing up the roof, or killing a larger animal that is prowling our territory and could be a danger, but we should try not to cause pain. If that animal is an endangered species, it would be better to capture it and release it back into the wild.

CANNIBALISM

Alfred Parker killed five of his companions and ate their flesh while stranded for the winter in the mountains of Colorado. This was murder and cannot be condoned. But if an airplane goes down in the cold north, and some are killed, and you are out of food, and you don't expect to be rescued for some time, should you eat the meat of the dead bodies? Why not? There is no logic to thinking that cannibalism is unacceptable. There should be no taboo. Neanderthals are known to have been cannibals, as are many animals.

We are animals, and our brains tell us that cannibalism would not be detrimental to our society. Eating a dead human is no different from leaving your body to medical research. When a warrior's brave enemy was killed by ancient man, he believed that by eating that enemy's flesh, he would add to his own strength and power.

Maybe we should hope that by eating our loved one, we would receive the strength of their love. Instead of burying our dead loved one, it would be better to have a celebration dinner in place of a memorial service. A eulogy could be given in place of the blessing. The children would like the braised brains, and the wife would want the highly sought-after penis on a bun.

FEWER LAWS AND LESS GOVERNMENT

We have too many laws and regulations in order to enforce all the unnecessary restrictions and 'must-dos'. We have too many civil servants, police and politicians. Taxes are high owing to our over-regulation. A reform commission should be set up to recommend the removal of outdated laws (we can still be charged with witchcraft) and the re-wording of many others, such as censorship laws. The commission should be empowered to make sure that its recommendations are brought before parliament.

What we need is a Minister of Pleasure whose job is to encourage the growth of pleasurable experiences for all, and ee's success would be measured by the nation's Gross National Pleasure.

The politician who gets elected again thinks the people liked what ee did, and the losers think that they did not please, but neither knows for sure which of their many actions were good or bad or whether the voter was voting for the nam or the party.

We should have a more participatory democracy, so the voice of the people can be heard. Politicians think they know what the people are thinking, because they talk to people, read the polls and receive letters. The number of people they actually talk to is small; the polls are not that good because too few people are surveyed; the questions are not always unbiased; and the letters are few.

Everyone should be asked for an opinion, so our leaders will know how we actually feel. This is not suggesting government by referendum. Leaders would not be expected to abide by the majority if ee felt ee had a better knowledge of the subject, but ee would know that more time should be spent on educating the people to ee's view.

The views of the people could be obtained by having questions on the ballot at each election. The number of questions could be divided among the parties according to the number of sitting representatives from each party. Each party would choose the wording of its allotted questions. Answering the questions on the ballot would not be mandatory, but almost everyone would if the questions had been published in advance. National referendum questions could also be added to yearly income tax forms.

We should have no laws concerning pornography, obscenity, sexual orientation, prostitution, nakedness, gambling, alcohol and drugs, including glue and gasoline for sniffing. It should not be the role of government to protect people from the consequences of pleasures they freely choose for themselves. Just think of the money to be saved.

We should not have laws that cannot be enforced or would be too expensive to enforce. We should not have laws relating to marriage or laws that would encourage and promote marriage and family. Just think, you would not have to try to define lesbian or homosexual couples. We should, however, have laws requiring firearms to be registered, just like cars.

Each jurisdiction has a building code, an electrical code, a book on driving regulations and many other code books. What we need badly is a book summarizing municipality by-laws, which should be updated regularly. We need a book on criminal law where one can look up the laws under a descriptive heading that would be a summary in a language understood by the majority of people. If we are going to say 'ignorance of the law is no excuse', we should make an effort to have the laws more available.

We can't expect the police to protect all of us from harm, and safety codes will not protect all of us. We couldn't afford 100% protection even if it were possible. We assume and know that we have a certain percentage chance of harm or death. In other words, we feel that life is precious, but not so precious that we will spend too much time and money on safety.

Our police force cannot always protect women from men. Even today, in countries like India, men sometimes kill female babies, circumcise the female clitoris, hit women, and divorce them by saying 'I divorce you.'

This is a social thing. Men are starting to listen to the cries of women and are starting to think that women should be treated equally, but there is a long way to go. In the meantime, women must learn to live with the danger of sexual harassment, rape, physical attacks and murder. The FBI say that 30% of the women murdered in the US each year are killed by their boyfriends or husbands. We have laws to punish those who do these things, but women should be prepared to defend themselves, at least to some degree. Remember, your brain is your best defence.

A car with doors locked or a house or apartment with doors and windows locked is fairly safe, but being out alone requires something more, such as a weapon, a spray, an alarm or even a small video camera. Women wearing high-heeled shoes show they are weak and vulnerable and cannot run away. They should wear steel-toed shoes that can immobilize a man with a kick to the testicles or shin.

A high percentage of our criminals come from poor home backgrounds. To reduce the carnage in the future, we should concentrate on having children brought up in sofraternities where professional facilities are available to keep all the children going happily in the right direction. Those who do not respond to rehabilitation should be punished as adults, and if they are convicted of first degree murder, they should receive the death penalty. It is just. It is right. It is economical.

Murderers have given up the right to life. Plunging the knife in or shooting where it could kill, is 'intent to kill' and, if caught and convicted of first degree murder, the death penalty should be mandatory. An armed robber who kills would know that the penalty for hei is death. If ee has been willing to gamble with ee's own quality of life, why should society insist on keeping hei alive? No matter how good a citizen ee has been, a murderer has committed suicide, and has no right to rehabilitation. The death sentence should be carried out by a quick and painless means. Gas, electrocution and hanging should not be used. Wouldn't it be nice if life were like a computer, so that when you make that big mistake you could have the whole thing erased.

It should not matter if the accused was drunk, on drugs, a battered child, influenced by TV or even insane. If ee did it, we don't want hei around. We certainly don't want hei to be able to write about it and get rich from the book and TV rights. If you find a rotten apple, you get rid of it, so it won't endanger the other apples, but you try to find out why it went bad, and try to handle the other apples so they won't go bad.

The legal system can and does make mistakes. If an accused is convicted and put to death and later found to be innocent, it is deplorable, but we live in a society where people are often killed due to other people's errors. Bridges and buildings fall down and kill, due to human error. We should try hard to avoid convicting innocent people, but we should not outlaw the death penalty. The alternative of incarceration for life at public expense is simply too expensive. Locking people up gives peace of mind but little else.

There are cases where the criminal should go to jail, but this should be the exception rather than the rule. Prison should be a place where no one would like to be. The food should be adequate and nourishing, but that's all. Smoking, liquor and drugs should be forbidden. There should be no conjugal rights. If the prisoner has any assets or income, they should be used to pay for ee's time in jail. The prisoner's income and assets should also be used to pay for property damaged or stolen goods, and victims should be compensated as well. To allow a killer, convicted of second degree murder, to take ee's own life would also require society to agree that quality of life was most important. The convicted killer would be deciding whether 25 years minimum in prison was acceptable.

Minor crimes should be dealt with by fines and work projects for the community. For serious crimes – manslaughter, robbery with violence and rape – and for punishments in between the death sentence and prison, the convicted should be permanently deported to an island far away from a mainland. There they can live among other deported violent people who are insensitive to the pain of others, and establish any social arrangement they want. This is like many in the animal world where a member of the clan is expelled to try surviving on ee's own.

The first on the island should be given the bare necessities for farming and hunting (no guns) and whatever is necessary to let them survive, including some medical supplies. They could be visited maybe once a year to drop off more criminals and a few supplies. If they perish, so be it. We should not go back to putting them in prisons.

Penalties should be very severe for offences motivated by hate, based on race, nationality, colour, religion, sex, age, mental or physical disability or sexual orientation. Penalties should also be severe where the offender has taken advantage of a position of trust to abuse or sexually abuse a dependent person. Sex offenders should be chemically treated with Luride, or something more permanent, to cut down on the testosterone level. A second conviction should require castration.

Should we not see the good in people who have done bad things? Well, yes, but not to reduce the penalty. Too often we tend to treat evil as a disease and criminals as poor unfortunates who have contacted an infection. If people go astray, it is true that our society is somehow to blame, and we should try to understand how it came about, and try to change things, but we should not spend too much time and money trying to rehabilitate our failures.

Anyway, our success rate is quite small, especially in a prison setting which just adds to the capacity for violence. Our time and money would be better spent by concentrating on the prevention of the disease by having special arrangements for children showing bad tendencies. This should be a standard arrangement in the sofraternities.

Everyone should be fingerprinted and photographed periodically for identification purposes, not only for a driving licence, but for work applications and restricted purchases, such as guns.

Our jury system is probably a good method, but too often the jurors assume that what an eyewitness remembers is a true picture of what happened, while tests have shown that memory can be faulty. Several people reporting the same incident quite often give several different accounts. Repressed memories brought to light should also be suspect, because these so-called memories may be thoughts absorbed from a therapist. If you can remember a dream, it points out that your dream is in your memory, and some people may recall that memory and not realize that it was a dream.

Evidence should be carefully analyzed, because things are not always what they seem. If you see a person's face that is upside-down to your own, you do not recognize even someone you know well. Many things happen that are attributed to 'pilot error', when actually the person has done everything according to the rules or instructions, as far as ee knows.

For instance, a husband was thought to have put the toilet paper roll in, with the loose end hanging on the outside instead of against the wall. He remembers being careful to do it correctly, so doesn't understand how it could get reversed, until one day, putting in a new roll, he noticed that the last three squares had been folded back over the roll in the gluing process to hold the last squares in place. Putting the roll in the holder with the free end on the outside would appear to be correct, but as soon as the end was pulled, and more than three squares removed, the free end remaining would be against the wall. The moral of this story is that you should not rely on one piece of evidence, because it could be fallible.

No amount of training and/or hunting will get you a desirable job if there are no jobs available, so we do need some social assistance. This should be available from government, where all people share in the care-giving by contributing through taxes.

There should be only one financial social service, and that should be handled by a negative income tax system. It would save millions of dollars by doing away with all other financial assistance programmes. It shouldn't matter whether you are rich or poor in property, goods or investments, if your income is below the prescribed level, you pay no income tax. You would receive make-up income to bring you up to the prescribed level, well below the minimum wage.

If a nam is rich but in that year is unemployed and has little income from investments, ee would receive the make-up income. The logic in this is that ee has already paid income tax in the previous years, and it was only the money left over that ee used to buy the property, car, boat or art. To live above the prescribed level, ee could cash some investments or sell some property, which would not be classed as income.

Tax on income should be the only tax. We should have no sales tax or property tax. Each level of government – city, province or state, and federal – would set its tax rate to be applied to an individual's income and collected once a year with one tax form. There would be no hidden taxes, so your tax level should be quite evident. You and the government could easily discuss the level.

The rationale for this is that governments should not be concerned with how people spend their money. They should only be interested in their level of income. Whether people spend their money on food, cars, houses, spouses, children or philanthropy shouldn't matter.

For the same reason, tax forms should not have deductions for union or professional dues, child-care, alimony, charitable donations and many other expenses. The tax form would then be easy enough to fill out by everyone. It wouldn't be pages long with a separate 40 page book to tell you how.

When people pay income tax, they should not have to pay an additional tax on the money left over. In other words we shouldn't have a sales tax. There should be no tax on manufactured goods, including cigarettes and liquor. Income tax is all we need. Just think of the savings in nam hours of work by both store owners and civil servants by not having a sales tax. Governments should only be interested in how much you make, not how you spend it.

We have an organization to handle income tax, and this would have to be expanded in order to check on incomes more carefully. A one tax system would eliminate the time-consuming and costly effort to collect the present multitude of taxes, and it would reduce our civil service costs by millions of dollars.

All of the money collected from gambling goes to the owners of the business (in many cases it's the government) who are allowed to subtract expenses, and then they are taxed on the remainder, because this is the store's profit (owners' income). If the gambler receives prize money (or winnings), ee should not be taxed on that as income, because the prize is like a purchased item. The money is used to buy a prize, just like buying something at the store. All the gamblers have, in a sense, purchased the prize, and given it to one individual.

The human animal is no longer a hunter-gatherer, getting ee's own food and making ee's own shelter. We live in a society where we must have a job in order to get money so we can purchase these necessities.

Certainly the work you do should be enjoyable to some extent, or give some satisfaction, because you will be working maybe half of your life. Actually if you live to be 80 years old you will have spent 20 years learning, 40 years doing, and 20 years retired. Your choices for the first 20 years are not so great, but the next half of your life is where you can make the best choices from the jobs available. Don't neglect the possible last 20 years. These could be the roughest if you don't prepare for them. Age is mind over matter. If you don't mind, it doesn't matter.

The government should not be in the business of trying to create jobs. That kind of socialism doesn't work too well, as witnessed by the failure of the Soviet Union. Government is not the generator of economic stability. Working people are. But government should be involved in services required by all, such as defence, police, laws, courts and jails, roads and tax collecting. All the government can do is create the best conditions for job-creation and retention, including training, international trade, investment in research and development, and prudent fiscal and monetary management. Unfortunately, our economy has gotten better at producing goods and services with fewer people, and unemployment is high, so this is another reason drastically to reduce our population.

Years ago public workers received less money than they would make if doing the same job in the private sector, but somewhere after 1960 their pay rose until now it is 15% higher than the equivalent in industry. It is interesting to note that it was after 1960 that governments no longer balanced the budget, and the debt began to skyrocket. The civil service unions should primarily be involved with establishing an equivalent job description and pay levels comparable to the private sector.

The national debt that most countries have shows that governments have become too involved in bolstering the economy and trying to provide too high a standard of living for all. Some people argue that government borrowing money is no worse than people borrowing money, but people borrow money to buy a house or start a business, and these are collateral. The government doesn't get the collateral.

Debt reduction should be a priority. When you stop and think that as long as there is a national debt, you, the tax-payer, are paying the interest on the debt. You realise that it's not the government's debt, but your debt. The money was paid to you in old-age pensions, unemployment benefits, social security, job retraining, an expanded airport, etc. You may not have personally asked for it, but you did receive it, and you did spend all the money you got.

The total of all direct government, federal and provincial indebtedness (April 1995) equals $780 billion (Canadian) ($580 billion Federal and $200 billion Provincial). If our population is 30 million, each Canadian's portion of the debt is over $25,000 ($19,000 Federal and $6000 Provincial). It's like having a mortgage. You should pay it off as soon as you can, a little each year at least, in order to get rid of the big interest payments.

Do you realize that 33% of our tax dollar goes to pay the debt interest. A Canadian pays $3 in taxes and ee gets back only $2 in federal programs, subsidies and grants. Having to pay interest on a debt that is not earning income is a most wasteful way of throwing away money. It's your debt. Pay it off, and then try to make sure that the government doesn't continue its over-spending ways.

The government is promising to reduce the deficit in five years. They are not talking about the debt. They are talking about the deficit, the difference between the money they take in and the larger amount they give out to you and me.

The federal deficit for 1995–96 came in at 28.6 billion Canadian dollars. This is the amount added to the debt in just one year. Believe it or not, in that five years the debt will have increased, and our total debt will then be almost 1 trillion dollars. (The US debt in 1996 stood at $4.7 trillion and rising.) Get rid of the debt now.

An organization should be set up to start a fund-raising campaign, nationwide, asking us to contribute money or donate our Canada Savings bonds to a Bond Burning Ceremony to help pay off our debt. Bob Blair of Calgary has said it is time to bring back the idea of the Victory Bonds that were used to finance World War Two. Tim Paleczny of Toronto has suggested a 'debt trust fund' to give everyone an opportunity to assume a share of the cost of paying off the debt. You pay taxes to the government and they turn around and use your tax dollar to pay you interest on your bond. In other words we pay the government to pay us interest.

If you had a bank, trust, or Canada Savings bond earning a yearly interest, and then transferred it to the government so it could pay off a portion of the national debt, the government would not need to use tax money to pay the paid-off debt interest. Therefore, the government should allow you to reduce your tax by an amount that would leave you with the same amount of money after taxes as you would have had if you had received the bond interest. The government receives less taxes by the amount of interest it no longer has to pay. Your standard of living remains the same, but the national debt is reduced.

An advertising campaign should be launched to get people to contribute to the 'Ban The Bond' and 'Reduce The Debt' fund. People give to all sorts of worthwhile causes: public TV broadcast stations, universities, the United Way, but our debt is the greatest calamity Canada has ever had, greater than the damage from floods in Manitoba and Quebec, mine disasters, hurricanes, tornadoes and earthquakes. So people should be convinced that the debt is a worthwhile cause. In fact, the resulting reduction in taxes would be the most effective charity. Just think, if our debt is paid off, our taxes could be reduced by one-third. Back the attack.

Each town could have a target amount with a bar-graph at City Hall to show how much money is contributed. People's names could be published in the newspaper, like they are for the Star Fresh Air Fund. Older people would be encouraged to will a portion of their estate to the debt reduction. After all, the debt was mostly created by giving them money over the years since the 1960s. Every four dollars contributed would be a one dollar saving for the nation because of the interest reduction. People have been living beyond their means on their 'collective credit card'. Now is the time to pay up. Make the debt reduction a Millennium Project: Bond burning, December 31st 1999.

UNITED NATIONS TO GOVERN ALL

In the animal world, where there is a grouping you most often find a dominant male. In the human grouping, called a town or city, you have a town council. When several cities grow together, you find a metropolitan council. Each state or province has its elected council and each country has its leaders to organize the running of the country. It's not easy to run a country. Different areas desire and require different things, but if the people wish to have a successful country, they work it out. We have the North American Free Trade group and the European common market and other groupings, but the world is our biggest grouping, and it is only logical that the UN should be the arbitrator and government of all countries on earth, and should have its own military force.

MILITARY

The UN should be the arbitrator of disputes between countries, and it should have the power to control and enforce its laws. The UN could be a unifying force in many areas. There might be some difficulty in persuading some powers, such as the US, Britain, Germany and France, to eliminate their nuclear and conventional forces and leave the global protection job to the UN, but this must be the goal if anarchy is to end.

What is needed is a standing, potent and overwhelming force, loyal only to the UN. Its members would be selected for their devotion to a one-world ideal and an overwhelming desire to maintain peace and justice. All peoples of the world must be UN citizens so the multiple cultures and countries could be transformed into one planet-wide community, characterized by interconnecting needs and uniform services.

The savings on massive defence budgets would be tempting for all nations. If one group were fighting another group, the UN force could be used to stop the bloodshed and help bring about a peaceful solution. Some people were opposed to intervention in Yugoslavia, where many innocent people have been dying, on the grounds of national sovereignty. This is as out-of-date as police declining to stop family violence, simply because a man's home is his castle.

If dictators take control of a group of people where the majority do not want them, the United Nations should do all it can to force a change, including free elections. Invasion by military personnel would be used only if the UN is strong enough so that there is no chance of failure as in the Bay of Pigs. There ought to be no holding back, or a limited objective as in Vietnam or Korea.

Citizens in the country cannot expect their liberation to be free of civilian casualties, especially if the enemy uses them as shields. Many may pay the price for the freedom of their country. If the country in question is large or too strong, the UN should only use sanctions and isolation as weapons. We cannot try to save all people from a dictatorial ruler.

Do we need a UN force? Yes, we do, because unless absolutely everyone believes in peace, the few who don't will subjugate all the others.

The UN should promote the unification of a country. A new political party should be established in Israel, promoting the desire to create a unified country with a new name, such as 'Palrael', in which both Palestinians and Israelis would be citizens. Jerusalem would be the capital because it is the holiest city for both. The government would be as in other countries with a diverse population such as Canada, Belgium, Switzerland, etc. There would be two official languages, and people could live and work where they wished.

POLLUTION

The UN will control all things of a global nature, especially pollution which affects the whole world. Fishing and all tree-cutting and tree-planting should be regulated. Each country should be given a limit for the production of air pollution and water pollution where it affects the seas and oceans.

Population pollution is the greatest problem, and the UN must establish population goals for each country, depending on the country's ability to provide water, food and waste-disposal. The target population will keep changing with changing conditions, but the planned overall result would be to reduce the world population to 2 billion, or whatever is agreed upon.

If countries do not reach their target population for that year, no food-aid will be sent if they have a crop failure, unless the crop failure is more severe than they could have handled with the prescribed fewer people. Closing of the borders and some type of blockade might also be used. They should also realize that they can't take care of their over-population by letting people emigrate to other countries. Contraception and family-planning would help in a country's efforts to reduce its population.

IMPROVE AND STANDARDIZE

The UN should be a unifying body to promote standards throughout the world. Traditions handed down to us from our ancestors must be examined, and, if the old is cumbersome or not working well in the society of today, change can be made as long as a much better form or arrangement can be found.

When clocks kept reasonably good time, but no-one knew what time it was in the neighbouring town or country, a Canadian got everyone to agree to time zones, starting at Greenwich, England. When daylight-saving-time was adopted, it caused quite a stir. Clothing, shoe sizes and SOS as a distress signal became standardized. When airport controllers found that there were too many planes to handle safely, they got all airports to adopt a new reliable system and standardized to one language.

For some years the electric utilities had been supplying homes with 25-cycle current that caused light bulbs to flicker. You can imagine the cost and confusion when they changed to the more economical 60-cycle current and had to change every motor-driven appliance free of charge. Why continue with the old if it is cumbersome and causing problems? Make one of the following your twenty-first century project.

Science and technology is logic put to use. Our society is far beyond the one-nam-inventor in ee's workshop. It is the chemical and electrical laboratories and industrial giants that will produce the big changes in our future way of life. The average person must keep up with the new, in order to help decide which is good, safe and desirable. The only way to get that knowledge is through language and communication.

INTERNATIONAL LANGUAGE

The inhabitants of our planet use 5000 different languages, creating great difficulty in communicating properly.

A universal language should be developed through the UN, with the help of United Nations Education, Science and Culture Organization (UNESCO), so all people would have only one language to learn other than their own. Then all people could talk to one another in a common language. For many centuries nem have expressed the hope that the curse of Babel, the confusion of tongues, would someday be remedied.

Each period in our history has had a dominant language. There were Greek and Latin, and later the French language was dominant. Even the British used French for foreign correspondence and discussions until England became successful with their overseas colonies. When the French lost battles at Waterloo and in North America, the English language became more dominant. After two world wars, Korea, Vietnam, and the seven-day-war against Iraq, the English language has become the undisputed dominant language, but still it is only spoken by maybe 15% of the world's population.

All through history, when several language groups became

governed by one group, it wasn't too long before only one language was used. This was logical and inevitable, because it would be so cumbersome to have more than one language. North America was settled by German, French, Dutch, Spanish and many other language groups, and all tried to promote their particular language. English became dominant, and before long the others gave in, except in Quebec. In the British Isles, you had Norsemen, Romans, and others, but it finally came down to Gaelic and English. It's not convenient to run a country with more than one language, so it wasn't long before English won out.

Language groups are protective of their language and culture, so much so that in many cases fighting breaks out. It is argued that wars take place because people do not understand one another, and language is seen as the chief cause. In Yugoslavia you have the Croats fighting the Serbs (Muslims). In Canada you have the French-speaking Quebec people trying to break away from the surrounding English.

All over the world smaller language groups had to adapt to the language of the dominant group in order to survive economically. You can't work with others unless you can communicate properly. That was true when you only had to communicate within your group or country, but today with radio, television, satellites in the sky, computers linked to every country, and everything happening instantaneously, your group is now the world. You know that a universal language will come, so we should start developing a good one now.

Some people feel that although language difficulties do occur, existing procedures are not totally unworkable, so their support for an international language is not an urgent priority, but it certainly should be. In the future, on the Information Highway, the dominant interface will be speech, and all people will have to use a common language, and it must be flawless or better than English. An international language would be such a great help for commercial and technical groups. Its use would break down the walls between nations and races and contribute to international understanding, inter-cultural appreciation, human brotherhood and world peace. An international language must come, and soon.

The UN headquarters in New York City spends millions of dollars per year to employ 315 translators and interpreters to translate from and into only seven languages: Arabic, Chinese, English, French, German, Russian and Spanish. The possibility of error and misunderstanding is great. The majority of delegates must constantly feel their minority status because they don't have their own interpreters. English-speaking people seem to be as insensitive to this discrepancy as they are incapable of accepting bilingualism themselves. They feel that English is already an international language and would be the hardest to convince that we need a better international language.

You may think that English would logically become the accepted international language, but it won't, because the other language groups will not give in. It would be resented as cultural imperialism. The nationalistic feelings of former colonies, such as India, Pakistan, Africa, and oriental countries, would not permit English, because they do not want to be reminded of their former colonial status, and for many it just means Hollywood. Why should everyone else have to learn a foreign language, when the English-speaking world would not? Besides, English is such a difficult language to learn.

How often have we heard improper use of English on the radio, TV and in everyday conversation, and wished we had a simpler language. There are so many words having several meanings; the spelling is not phonetic (fonetik) and has so many weird spelling arrangements; a letter has a variety of sounds depending on the word; grammar is sufficiently complicated that few get it right. We don't need separate words for subject and predicate as we have now, such as 'he' and 'him'.

There are people like Hans Eberstark, a linguistic genius, who can read and speak almost every language, and can even use many dialects and accents of each language. This is possible, to some extent, because almost all languages can be boiled down to find a universal grammar.

We might think that in making an international language it would be difficult to choose one word for an object or meaning out of all the different words in all the different languages. But Hans points out that in so many cases there is a common root that they all came from, so selecting words for the UN language would not be an insurmountable task. Selecting a word for an object or idea or making up a new word for the object would be a matter of selecting the most-used word or making a combination of the most-used words.

The UN should hire as many linguistic geniuses as it can find and request that each make up a new language with more letters in the alphabet, like the Russians, in order to have a letter for all the different sounds we make in speech. The new language should be easy to learn and speak; be logical in construction; be phonetic in pronunciation and spelling; be simple in grammar with few grammatical rules and no exceptions; have no gender, race or religious connotation, e.g. 'mailman'; have no irregularities and superfluous complications; be adaptable for adding new words.

Some people have an aversion to the idea of an artificial language, but a neutral second common language for mankind need not be a cultural language. A planned, constructed language is like 'artificial' ice, it lacks the twigs and other debris often found in 'natural' ice. There is no reason why a good UN language could not express feelings and be used in poetry and science, and be as beautiful as a cultural language. A good example of this is the well established, and already highly successful constructed language, Esperanto. This existing language should also be considered by the linguistic committee of the UN.

The best, or combination of the best, would be called the UN language. It would be made into a dictionary and distributed to each country, a different edition for each language group. School children, already over-burdened, would need to learn only two languages, their own plus the UN language starting in an early grade and continuing through all the following years. Young people entering the work-force, would use the UN language when communicating with a young foreign person, and use an interpreter to communicate with an older person who has not learned the UN language. Eventually everyone would be using it to talk to people outside their own language group.

Aeroplane pilots would be using it, and UN meetings would not need simultaneous translators. Tourists would all be using it to get food and train schedules, etc., because the host country would have bilingual cards everywhere in both the native language and in the UN language. Newspapers would be published in two editions; packaged food products would have information in two languages, just like in Canada.

Native peoples could keep their own language and culture, but they would now be able to communicate with outsiders without having to learn other native languages. Just think of the difference it would have made if the French in Quebec could have talked to the English without having to condescend to use the English language. They probably would not now be considering a separation from Canada.

An international authority is needed around which people can build new identifications and supra-national loyalties. The UN will eventually be that unifying force for land, sea, air and space.

CALENDAR

The UN should be in the forefront for promoting standardizations in areas that affect all people of the world. If an existing standard is clumsy or difficult to use, the UN should promote a change to a better standard.

Our calendar is one of those things that should be changed. It is not sacrosanct. It is not a convenient tool. It's a mish-mash handed down to us after having been changed many times. The major problem is that it is so difficult to use. It binds us to a seven day week that cannot be evenly divided into our month. The months do not have the same number of days, and the days do not fall on the same date each year.

One always has to have the present year's calendar at hand to find out what dates will be the last weekend in a particular month; what day of the week a certain calendar day is; what day of the week your birthday falls on; what dates your holiday will fall on. And you need next year's calendar to figure out what dates would be suitable for next year's holiday. To remember the number of days in each month, one has to remember the verse, 'Thirty days hath September, April, June and November. All the rest have thirty-one except February, etc.'

We need a calendar that you can keep in your head, which would be the same every year, and each date would always be associated with the same day of the week. The 13 month calendar would look like this:

13 Month Calendar

S	M	T	W	T	F	S
1	2	3	4	5	6	7
8	9	10	11	12	13	14
15	16	17	18	19	20	21
22	23	24	25	26	27	28

That's all there is. There ain't no more.

Before we look at the advantages of a new calendar, we should understand how we ended up with the Gregorian calendar we have today. Early nam started to count the number of 'suns' (days) that a journey took, and for longer trips the number of full moons (the word month comes from moon).

Early calendars were based on the moon's cycle of 29 and a half days. To have a month made up of days that would keep in phase with the moon's cycle, they used a series of months with 30, 29, 30, 29 days each, but every three years they would have to add a month to keep in phase with the seasons, because six months of 30 days plus six months of 29 days equals 354 days. This is 11 days short of a full season which they knew consisted of 365 days (the time the earth takes to make one complete journey around the sun).

The next big change came when they stopped using the moon's cycle to divide up the year. The ancient people were exceptionally familiar with the stars and planets, and had given names to many star constellations. When the Egyptians noticed that there were 12 evenly-spaced constellations which appeared to rotate around the horizon in one year, they changed the calendar to make each month 30 days long.Thirty times 12 equals 360 days, which is only five days per year short of 365, so they added five days at the end of each year as festival days. What a bash that must have been.

Actually the time the earth takes to go around the sun is not exactly 365 days. It is approximately 365 and a quarter days.

When the Roman ruler Julius Caesar became dominant, he established the Julian calendar to keep the year from slipping behind. The calendar was to have 12 months, six months of 31 days, alternating with five months of 30 days, and February was to have 29 days, with a day added to February every four years to make up the quarter day.

Unfortunately, because Julius Caesar had named the seventh month after himself (July), his successor Augustus Caesar decided to name the eighth month after himself (August), and because July had 31 days, Augustus had August changed to 31 days also. Other months were changed so that the Julian calendar ended up with four 30-day months (30 days hath September, April, June and November), and seven 31-day months, while February had 28 days, with an additional day every four years.

Where did the other names come from? Back before Julius Caesar, the Romans began their year in the spring, and named their first month Martius (March) after their god Mars. Aprilis (April) had the meaning 'to open'; Maia (May) was the goddess of growth; Juno (June) was the goddess of marriage. After July and August the months were simply numbered with the Latin for 7 to 10 (septem,octo, novem, decem). The next 59 days of winter were left unnamed, but later became January and February. When our year started in January, the months September, October, November and December became our ninth to twelfth months, so the names now don't match the numbers.

The Julian calendar lasted until it was discovered that a year is not exactly 365 and a quarter days. By 1582 it was out by ten days, so Pope Gregory introduced the Gregorian calendar which we use today. It has a leap year every four years except those years ending in two zeros and not divisible by 400. Thus 1700, 1800 and 1900 were not leap years, but the year 2000 and 2400 will be.

Where did the week come from? The farmers required several days within the month to bring their products to market, but meat, vegetables and fruits would not stay fresh too long. The word 'week' was the word for 'market'. Four day and up to ten day weeks have been used, but eventually seven days became standard, probably because the number seven was special; seven virtues; seven deadly sins; seven gods of happiness in Japan;

seven hills of Rome; and seven heavenly bodies (Sun, Moon, Mercury, Venus, Mars, Jupiter and Saturn); and the Jewish seventh day of rest.

Three days of the week are named after heavenly bodies; the sun for Sunday; the moon for Monday; Saturn for Saturday. The other names come from gods of our Anglo-Saxon heritage; Tiw for Tuesday; Woden for Wednesday; Thor for Thursday; and Frigg for Friday.

Each calendar change was traumatic, but was done to make the calendar more logical and useful. When we make a change, it will take some getting used to, but it will be worth it. A calendar change would be no more of a problem for school children or adults than changing to the metric system was in Canada.

We are used to showing the date as 2/6/97, so we really don't need to use the old out-dated names for the months. We should merely call them by their logical numbers: month one, month six, etc. 'See you on the twelfth of month seven' would probably eventually be shortened to 'See you on the twelfth of seven.'

Because we are used to saying 'March 6th', many people and businesses denote this as 3/6/95, for example, but the International Organization of Standardization recommends numerical dating by year, month and day to be consistent with the military way. The UN must establish a standard. But we will probably still use the Sunday to Saturday names for the seven days of the week, just because we are so used to them.

The 13 month calendar is as good as you can get for dividing up a year that does not have an equal number of days. Primarily it is so easy to remember and use. People will easily remember that the first day of the month always falls on Sunday, so days one and seven will always be Sunday and Saturday respectively, and the numbers in-between will be the other days of the week. Most people will be able to remember that Mondays will be on the second, ninth, sixteenth, and twenty-third. If they don't remember, all they need to do is add a series of sevens to Monday's day two to arrive at nine, sixteen and twenty-three. You will always know the weekend dates, and the calendar will be the same for every month and every year in the future. That's it! If only vacuuming the living room were that quick and easy.

In order to accommodate leap year, February would have a 29th day every leap year, but it would not have one of the regular week day names. It would be called 'Leapday' and be a holiday to make a long weekend in between Saturday and Sunday. Because 13 times 28 is only 364 days, an extra day would come after the 28th day of Month 13 and be a holiday called 'Yearday'. This would make a long weekend for the New Year celebration.

There is another suggested calendar called the World Calendar which has 12 months with equal quarters of a year by having a series of 31, 30, and 30 days. The business need for equal quarters probably no longer exists, because computers are so flexible, but if it is needed, the 13 month calendar can easily be divided into equal quarters of a year as well. Thirteen weeks is exactly a quarter of 52 weeks, the same exactly as the World Calendar. So the simplicity and convenience of the 13 month calendar, sometimes called the International Fixed Calendar, should win out.

An ideal time to change to the 13 month calendar would be at the end of the present millenium after midnight Dec. 31, 2000. It might be a good idea at the same time to end the era of the A.D. Christian calendar numbering and have January 1st in the year 01 of the 13 month calendar.

METRIC

The UN should be involved in promoting the metric system of measurements as a standard for all nations. In the United States and many other parts of the world they are still using 12 inches to a foot, 3 feet to a yard, 5280 feet to a mile, 2 pints to a quart, 4 quarts to a gallon, 2000 pounds to a short ton, 2400 pounds to a long ton and 1 stone equals 14 pounds. All of this is so illogical and cumbersome. It's no wonder kids have trouble in school. Measurements smaller than an inch, shown as fractions – 1/2, 1/4, 1/8, 1/16, 1/32 and 1/64 – are so difficult to work with.

The metric system is so simple and logical and easy to learn as there are no fractions. It is based on units divisible by 10 and in multiples of 10. A metre (slightly longer than a yard) is divided into 10 decimetres. A decimetre (not often used) is divided into 10 centimetres. A centimetre is divided into 10 millimetres, etc.

1,000 metres is one kilometre (deka- and hectometres are seldom used). Volume is measured in litres and weight is measured in grammes, both with the above prefixes.

Unlike the inch, quart and pound, the metre, litre and gramme are all inter-related. A cube, 10 centimetres on each side, equals 1 litre. A litre of water at 4 degrees Celsius weighs 1 kilogramme. The so-called Metric System also includes a standard for measuring temperature. When the old Fahrenheit scale was developed, it assumed 100 degrees was the temperature of the human body, and 0 degrees was the freezing temperature of any equal amount of salt and water. The metric Celsius scale has 100 degrees as the boiling temperature of water, and 0 degrees as the freezing temperature of water. Other standards include the second for time, the ampere for electric current and candle for luminous intensity.

The adoption in Canada of the metric system took a lot of time, money, effort, education and planning, but it paid off. We got into step with the majority of the world and became competitive in all the overseas countries. The children in school had to be taught the new system, and that took years, but before long even the older people were starting to use it. So many things had to be changed: lumber dimensions; nail sizes; tools to make the nuts and bolts that needed new threading dimensions, and all the road speed signs, but look at the good results. The United States has just again postponed starting their programme to convert to metric, but this time the postponement is permanent. Maybe when their economy improves, they will start their move to metric.

It may be interesting to note here that the metric 10 is based on the number of fingers we have on the total of both hands. Whoever thought up the idea of adding a nought to a one to represent the next number following the last-named number was clever, because doubling that becomes 20 etc., and 10 times 10 equals 100. So simple to use. The nought is also used to represent nothing, zero, not anything, the absence of quantity.

If people had been used to counting only on the left hand, the nought could have been added to 1 to represent the thumb, and we would have a metric system counting: l, 2, 3, 4, 10, 11, 12, 13, 14, 20, 21, etc. In other words, 10 can be used to represent any quantity of items we like.

In fact 10 can be used to represent the number after one. If we only had one finger on each hand, we might have been counting so that one finger would be 1 and the other finger would be 10. This method is used in calculators and computers. These devices use transistors that are electrical devices that allow current to flow or prevent current flowing. In other words, like an electrical switch, it is either on or off. If we represent 'off' by 0 and 'on' by 1, we can arrange for it to count using only zeros and ones (computer metric).

Standard Metric	Computer Metric	Dozenal Metric
0	0	0
1	1	1
2	10 (ten)	2
3	11	3
4	100	4
5	101	5
6	110	6
7	111	7
8	1000	8
9	1001	9
10 (ten)	1010	✠
11	1011	☆
12	1100	10 (ten)
13	1101	11
14	1110	12
15	1111	13
16	10000	14

Dozenal Metric

one	two	three	four	five	six	seven	eight	nine	ses	des	ten
1	2	3	4	5	6	7	8	9	✠	☆	10
11	12	13	14	15	16	17	18	19	1✠	1☆	20

eleven sixteen sesteen desteen

If our ancestors had been born with six fingers on each hand, we would probably have been counting by dozenal metric, where 10 would represent the number of fingers we would have had on the total of both hands. Six would be half of 10. The dozenal metric would have been better than standard metric, because the standard 10 can be divided only by 1, 2 and 5, whereas the dozenal metric 10 can be divided by 1, 2, 3, 4 and 6. This is handy when you want to package items in quantities of 10, so that all you have to do is count the packages (like 18), and then add a zero to that number (180) to have the total number of items in all the packages. With the dozenal metric, you would be able to have more packaging arrangements.

With the dozenal metric, we could also have a metric clock. We wouldn't need a.m. and p.m. because the afternoon hours would be the same as the morning hours except with a 1 in front.

20
10

19 9   3 13

6
16

When the international language is established, the words for the numbers may not be on the English language basis, but if they are, the words should be improved to be more logical. The word 'ten' should be replaced by 'onety' to go with 'onety-one', 'onety-two', etc., 'twoty', 'threety', 'forty', 'fivety', 'sixty', 'seventy', 'eighty', 'ninety'.

Ah well, it's just enjoyable to try to figure things out. Have fun.

Enjoy yourself
Enjoy yourself
It's later than you think.

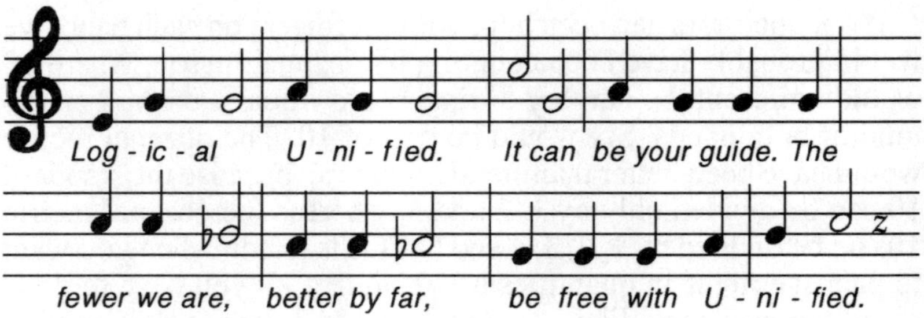
Log - ic - al U - ni - fied. It can be your guide. The
fewer we are, better by far, be free with U - ni - fied.

CONCLUSION

We have pleaded with the enemy to stop the child-birth explosions that could kill us all, but no such undertaking has been received and consequently this country is at war with population. All nations are under attack, so we must combine our forces of contraception including condoms, the pill and the most powerful weapon, abstinence. This is World War Three. It will be long and hard, but we can win if people use the logic outlined in the Unified Life Theory.

This theory suggests that: we are merely animals; there is no reason to believe we are sacred or divine, and must protect every living soul for the glory of God; the nuclear family should become few in number so that children can be brought up by professionals in sofraternity type accommodations; sex and romance will become far less important as people become more involved with daily activities and achievements; money and lives can be saved by reducing all the censorship laws and therefore having fewer people in prison; taxes can be reduced by 1/3 if we pay off our national debt.

Women must take control of their professional, personal and sexual lives, decide what population numbers are best for humans and make it happen. The women's movement should adapt the word "unified' as their clarion call, 'All for one and one for all'.

When the war is won, the United Nations will become a central unifying force, a governing body over all nations with a military larger than individual countries. It will make life much simpler and safer by establishing standards throughout the world.

The Unified Life Theory will prove to be the saviour of mankind as well as the other animals and insects of the world, and living will be more enjoyable.

APPENDIX 1: A BRIDGE BIDDING CONVENTION

When you see something that you think should be improved, take time to try to figure out a better solution. There is a great deal of pleasure in the trying, and, if you succeed, it is a wonderful feeling. Don't be discouraged by people who say, 'If there were a better way, the experts would have found it.' This has been proven wrong so many times. Here is an example.

In bridge, all bidding methods use conventions where a bid is made to give information that has nothing to do with the suit bid. Conventions are designed so that you and your partner can try to describe your hands to each other in order to decide what contract to be in, if any. There is no bidding method that can describe the make-up of the hands exactly, and none can ever give all of the important features. Some, developed by super-brained experts, can describe a large number of features, but the method is most complicated and requires the ability to remember a large number of rules for the many possible situations.

The most important features to discover are: total count; the suits in which you have a total of 8 cards or more, and if one hand has a much larger number; and whether both hands are balanced to consider NT (no trump). So a good idea would be to design a bidding method so that the first bid of both you and your partner would show your total count; the next bid would show the number of cards held in a particular suit, etc. The following isn't perfect, but you will find that it is the best system for finding the features of your combined hands that are most important to discover.

First Round Count Convention

This convention assumes you have a general knowledge of the Gorin or Standard American bidding procedure, and that you have some experience playing the hand. But if you find you can't remember all the bidding rules laid out in a great big book, take heart, the bidding convention laid out in these few pages is easy to learn and remember, because logical explanations are given for each rule.

The combined hand count (A=4, K=3, etc.) and the combined number of cards in a suit of you and your partner is most important. Every bid you make, using the FRCC, will be a 'Q bid', giving information but having no relationship to the suit actually bid, until a game contract is bid, 3NT, 4♥, 4♠ or slam. Please note that ♣ and ♦ are not considered in the first phase of FRCC bidding, because a 3NT bid would be preferred to a 5♣ or a 5♦ bid. A contract in ♣ or ♦ should be most unusual except in a part-score or slam bidding (same as Standard American).

After you and your partner have each bid once (see Table 1 and Table 2 under FRCC BIDDING (see below), you will both know that your combined hand count is either: not enough to bid game; enough to bid game in ♥, ♠ or NT; enough to bid game in ♣ or ♦; enough to bid a little slam; or enough to bid a grand slam.

The next bid by opener (see Sequence 1) will show the number of cards in a particular biddable suit (any 4 card suit is biddable). The next bid by the responder (see Sequence 2) will show whether ee has support or not. Ee has support if ee has the number of cards in that suit which, when combined with opener's number of cards, totals 8 cards (Golden Fit) (same as Standard American). You may then bid a game in that suit. When a game bid is made in a suit or NT, this is recognized as a true bid and not a Q bid. That's all there is to it as long as you can count – well, almost.

The following is a more detailed procedure for using the FRCC. Determine your hand count by using Gorin's high card points: A=4, K=3, Q=2 and J=1. Also use Standard American distribution points: 1 point for every card over 4 in a suit. The hand count is the same whether you are thinking of a suit or NT (same as Standard American).

FRCC BIDDING

Table 1

Your team's opening bidder bids:

	Count =	13–14	15–16	17–18	19–20	→	31–32
If opponents have *not* bid,	Bid =	1♣	1♦	1♥	1♠	→	2NT
If opponent's bidding is at level 1 or is at a raised or weak 2 level,	Bid =	Double	+1	+2	+3	→	+9

If opponent's bidding is at level 2 (not a raised or weak 2), or at a pre-empt 3 or higher, do *not* use FRCC.

Table 2

Your team's responder bids, if your team's opener used FRCC:

		If opponent on right has passed; Bid	If opponent on right has doubled re-doubled or *not* bid over +4: Bid
If combined hand count is	13→18	Pass	Pass
Not enough for game	19→25	+1	Double or Redouble
Game in ♥ or ♠	26→28	+2	+1
Game in ♣ or ♦	29→32	+3	+2
Little slam	33→36	+4	+3
Grand slam	37→	+5	+4

Sequence 1

If a ♥ or ♠ has *not* been shown by partner:

Bid = +1 = *No* 4 card ♥ or ♠, or hand is suitable for NT, or proceed with next bid.

+2 = 4♥ or have support for original suit.

+3 = 4♠

+4 = 5♥

+5 = 5♠

+6 = 6♥

+7 = 6♠

+8 = 7♥

+9 = 7♠

Sequence 2

If a ♥ or ♠ has been shown by partner:

Bid = +1 = Do *not* have support for suit shown and do *not* have Other Major Suit (OMS) to show.

+2 = Support for suit shown and do *not* have 4 card OMS.

+3 = 4 OMS

+4 = 5 OMS

+5 = 6 OMS

+6 = 7 OMS

If opponents show a strong hand, your chances of having enough total count for game are not great, so do *not* open using FRCC (use Gorin or Standard American) if your opponents open the bidding with a 'Strong 2' bid, or a pre-emptive 3 bid or higher, or if your opponent has opened and your partner has passed and your opponent's responder has bid a new suit or NT at level 2 (but not a raised 2) or higher. If you are the first of your team to open the bidding using FRCC (you have a count of 13 or more) bid according to your hand count (see Table 1).

Where a +1 or +2 etc. is shown, +1 means bidding 'up 1'. If the previous bid is 1♥, +1 means you are to bid 1♠, and +2 means bidding 'up 2'. If the previous bid is 1♣, +2 means you are to bid 1♥.

The responder would continue using FRCC if the opponent on ee's right has passed, doubled, re-doubled or not bid over +4. If the opponent bids higher than that, your chances of having enough count for the game are not as great, so the responder would continue bidding using Gorin or Standard American, and you would too. You now do not know your partner's exact count, but ee knows yours and should be able to guide your bidding.

The reason for not always using FRCC when opponents are bidding is that if you and your partner take bidding space to show count only, the bidding could reach a higher level than desired before even showing a suit.

To continue FRCC, the responder adds ee's hand-count to yours and bids according to Table 2, based on the following:

A total count of 19 = enough to bid and make 1 in a suit
A total count of 21 = enough to bid and make 2 in a suit or 1NT
A total count of 23 = enough to bid and make 3 in a suit or 2NT
A total count of 26 = enough to bid and make 4 in a suit or 3NT
A total count of 29 = enough to bid and make 5 in a suit or 4NT
A total count of 33 = enough to bid and make 6 in a suit or 6NT
A total count of 37 = enough to bid and make 7 in a suit or 7NT

If the responder bids to show 'not enough for game', you both continue using Gorin or Standard American.

If your partner opens showing a count of 25–26, the responder bidding +1 no longer means 'not enough for game', because the opener has enough for game in ee's hand. Therefore, the responder bidding +1 would now mean 'game in ♥ or ♠' and +2 would mean 'game in ♣ or ♦', etc. If your partner opens showing 33–34, the responder bidding +1 would mean 'can't do better than little slam,' while +2 would mean enough for grand slam.

There are only two sequences to use for the rest of the FRCC bidding. The first sequence is to be used when a suit has not been shown by your partner. Your team's opening bidder would use Sequence 1. The responder would use Sequence 1 if the opener bids +1 (no 4 card major), or Sequence 2 if the opener bids +2 or more (showing a suit). Continue using Sequence 1 and 2 until you are ready to bid a game contract including 3NT. All bids are Q bids until a game contract is bid in a suit or NT. You are no longer bidding FRCC after that.

After establishing total count, the opener's next FRCC bid will be as per Sequence 1, to show a biddable suit. Show the shortest suit first and show ♥ before ♠ if they are of the same length. You will see the reason for this in Sequence 1 where you go up twice as fast for the first suit shown, compared with the Other Major Suit (OMS) on a subsequent bid as per Sequence 2. ('Show' in this context indicates the suit being referred to when a Q bid is made.)

A biddable suit is one that has 4 cards of any denomination. The number of high cards (A,K,Q,J) in the suit is not considered at this stage (same as Standard American). This is also true for the responder who, when showing support, does not consider the number of high cards in the suit.

It is important to have a second suit shown immediately, so if the responder has a biddable OMS (4 card), ee should show it before ee shows that ee can't (+1), or can (+2), support the opener's shown suit. Support means the responder has the number of cards in that suit which, when added to the opener's number of cards, totals 8 (Golden Fit).

If the responder shows support (+2) for the opener's first shown suit, the opener should consider bidding the OMS if ee's suit is biddable. But remember, the responder has not only said ee supports the opener's suit, but also ee says ee does *not* have 4 cards in the OMS which ee would have shown rather than showing support at this stage. Therefore, there is no point in the opener showing a 4-card OMS, because ee knows the responder does not have 4 to make a total of 8. To be biddable, the opener's OMS must now have 5 cards, and ee should show it in case the responder has 3 cards. If the responder does then show support (+2) for the OMS, the opener can now choose to bid the game in either suit. The best suit is the one with the largest number of cards in the two hands, but it is best also to have as many cards in one hand as possible. All things being equal, choose the suit with the most high cards, if known.

If the responder does not show support for the opener's first shown suit, but shows the OMS (+3 or more) if you (the opener) have support, you bid +2, or if you don't have support, you bid +1. In any case the responder then bids +2 if ee has support for the original suit, and +1 if ee doesn't.

The opener may then decide to bid +1 (Sequence 1 = proceed with next bid) or make a meaningless bid, such as +2 or +3 to ask the responder to choose. If the opener bids +1 or makes a meaningless bid, this can be used to let the partner be the first to bid the Golden Fit suit, so ee can be the declarer with the stronger hand (unless the suit has been bid in the Q bidding). The responder knows that +2 or +3 are meaningless bids in this case, because of having already shown support and because you cannot bid another suit. You are allowing the responder to be the declarer.

If either partner has 8 cards in ♥ or ♠ in the one hand, preferably with a number of high cards, that partner can immediately bid to game (if the count is enough for game).

Once a suit has been selected, the responder may re-evaluate ee's hand using dummy points (1-3-5) to see if sufficient points are available for slam.

In some cases (maybe when opponents are bidding) if a Golden Fit has been found there will not be bidding room to search for another in the OMS, so the bidder should bid the game in the Golden Fit already found.

If a Golden Fit is found in one suit and you are bidding to see if you have a Golden Fit in the other suit, you may have to make a

Q bid of 3NT, but your partner will know this is not a game bid, because you have already shown a Golden Fit in the first suit. A contract of 4♥ or 4♠ is preferred to 3NT (same as Standard American).

After both have indicated that no Golden Fit exists in ♥ or ♠, each should bid +1 (Sequence 1) if their hand is suitable for NT and then bid 3NT. If a hand is not best suited to NT, and if the total count is known to be 29 → 32 points (enough for the game in a minor suit), and if the hand has a strong 6 card or more ♣ or ♦ suit, continue bidding Sequence 1 and 2, but substitute ♣ for ♥ and ♦ for ♠, and now +2 (sequence 1) would not show 4♣ but would show 6♣, (4♣ if count is 33 or more) etc. If the count is less than 30, you may still use this system if hands are not suitable for NT, but don't bid over 4.

If the count of both hands totals 33 or more, enough for slam, use FRCC to find a Golden Fit first in ♥ or ♠ and then in ♣ or ♦, or choose NT. After support has been shown, if bidding space allows, +1 requests Aces to be shown, and after Aces are shown, +1 requests Kings to be shown (+1 = 0A, +2 = 1A, etc.).

You and your partner should agree on Q bids and sequences. You may wish to make changes to suit your own style.

APPENDIX 2: TWO HANDED BRIDGE

The Bid 2 Play 2 Method

Most methods are not sufficiently similar to real bridge to be satisfactory, but the Bid 2 Play 2 Method allows you to bid and play according to your regular systems. The only difference is that you have seen the contents of one other hand. Let's see how it works.

You and the *other person* sit opposite each other at the card table. If you are selected to be the dealer, you deal the usual four hands. Being the dealer you pick up the cards that are in front of you, bid the hand and lay the cards face down in front of you. The *other person* picks up the cards that are on ee's right, bids the hand and lays the cards face down on ee's right. The *other person* then picks up the cards that are in front of hei, bids the hand and lays the cards face down in front of hei. You then pick up the cards that are on your right, bid the hand and lay the cards face down on your right. The bidding continues in this fashion until one opposite pair wins the final contract. Note that you and the *other person* are always bidding as partners on each set of hands.

If the hand in front of you is the declarer, you play that hand, and the hand opposite will go down as your dummy, after the first lead. The first lead is made by the *other person* from the hand on ee's right. You play from the dummy and the *other person* then plays from the hand on ee's left. The *other person* is now your opponent playing the hands on both your right and your left. This gives the *other person* an advantage, because ee is allowed to view both hands at any time. You are expected to *not* remember what cards were in the hand on your right that you saw when bidding. The play continues until the contract is won or lost.

You could keep score ignoring the fact that the *other person* was your partner during the bidding, or you could keep a joint score, subtracting the defeated contract score from the fulfilled contract score.

If the hand on your right becomes the declarer you would play that hand with the hand on the *other person*'s right as the dummy. The *other person* would play the cards in front of hei plus the cards in front of you. This of course would be cumbersome, so it is best for both of you to move to the chair on your right, or preferably just move each set of cards clockwise one position.

Instead of picking up and laying the hands down, it is much better to make four boards to hold the cards. A board eight inches long and two inches wide with a slanted slot down the middle has been found adequate.

The second game would be dealt by the *other person* as if ee were dealing from the position on ee's right. The *other person* would make the first bid from that hand and then bid from the hand in front of hei. You would then bid from the hand on your right followed by a bid from the cards in front of you.

The third game would be dealt by the *other person* from ee's position opposite you. The fourth game would be dealt by you as if you were dealing from the position on your right, etc. Both of you deal and bid for the hands in front of you and the hands on your respective right. Both of you play the hand in front of you or the hand on your respective right when that hand becomes the declarer.

Have fun. Bridge is an enjoyable game.